THE COMPLETE ENTREPRENEURIAL GUIDE

THE small business PLANNER

to Starting and
Operating a
Successful
Small Business

LARRY WILSON

NEW YORK

THE Small Business PLANNER
THE COMPLETE ENTREPRENEURIAL GUIDE
To Starting and Operating A Successful Small Business

Larry Wilson

ISBN 978-1-60037-905-5 Paperback
ISBN 978-1-60037-906-2 Ebook
Library of Congress Control Number: 2010942276

Published by:

MORGAN JAMES PUBLISHING
The Entrepreneurial Publisher
5 Penn Plaza, 23rd Floor
New York City, New York 10001
(212) 655-5470 Office
(516) 908-4496 Fax
www.MorganJamesPublishing.com

Interior Design by:
Bonnie Bushman
bbushman@bresnan.net

In an effort to support local communities, raise awareness and funds, Morgan James Publishing donates one percent of all book sales for the life of each book to Habitat for Humanity.
Get involved today, visit
www.HelpHabitatForHumanity.org.

Thank you Ruth
for the many years of
inspiration and encouragement.

what people are saying

"I wish I had this invaluable tool ten years ago! The writing style is fast paced and congenial, not dry and distant, making the book readable. The templates are an excellent bonus – a nice way to get up and going faster with analysis work. As my children get more involved in the business, I think I'll make *The Small Business Planner* mandatory reading for them."

— **Todd Jones**, Furniture Retailer

"*The Small Business Planner* has been a valuable tool for the start up of my business. The author's clear, concise and to the point writing style allowed me to get the key points and save time doing so. As a startup, our time is our most valuable asset and the author well understands that. He has an excellent grasp of running a small business, especially when it comes to marketing, sales, and the Internet."

— **Steve Pallen**, President, Research and Development, *E-Metrotel*

"As a life-long entrepreneur, it was refreshing to finally have a user's guide to starting and operating a small business. The author looks at all facets of operating a business and breaks it down into small digestible pieces. This effective tool can be used by starting at the front cover or jumping right into any section, such as the excellent piece in Operations that focuses on creating effective web sites. One of the great qualities of *The Small Business Planner* is that the lessons can be implemented in any business; manufacturing, retail, service or the Internet. A must read for anyone starting a business or entrepreneurs who are looking for a refresher."

— **Mark Young**, MBA '97 U of T, President, Canadian Golf Tours Inc.

"The tips from the marketing section of the book such as budgeting and developing a strategy were invaluable for my business. The finance section was also so important as it made me realize how crucial measuring results on paper can be in making or breaking a seemingly successful business. I would highly recommend The Small Business Planner to anyone in the contracting business."

— **John Anderson**, Electrical Contractor

"In *The Small Business Planner*, Larry has provided all the tools necessary to help you market and promote, administer and track your business. The concepts are clearly explained and interspersed with his personal experiences, which make it easy to understand. This is a MUST read for those thinking of starting a small business and for those actively operating one."

—**Rick Scull**, Canadian Resurfacing Services Inc.

preface

This guide is ideal for anyone who is interested in starting a new enterprise as well as those who operate an established small business. My inspiration for writing *The Small Business Planner* came from work I was doing in government sponsored programs at business resource centers. Here I was fortunate enough to mentor entrepreneurs in the creation of business plans and marketing strategy for their start-up or existing business. Although there are numerous books available on the subject of entrepreneurship, according to the feedback I received from budding entrepreneurs enrolled in small business programs, most appeared to be written in terms foreign to the average new business owner. The available reference material also has a tendency to concentrate more on finance and less on marketing. Although sound financial management is critical to business success, it is the delivery of a solid marketing strategy that generates revenue. Of course, without revenue, there is no money to manage. *The Small Business Planner* covers finance in detail, but more than half of the book is dedicated to marketing and making money. The text books available to students for courses I taught at the college level also often fell short in this regard.

The market needed a guide for small business owners that was well organized, complete and understandable. I had written a regular column in a regional business newspaper called the *Small Business Planner* which covered a number of topics of interest to entrepreneurs from marketing and financial management to the creation of effective web sites. Originally, I intended to simply collect these articles for a new book, but then decided to include a great deal more information. After a year of research, re-writing and the inclusion of personal business experiences, a comprehensive guide, written in terms that are understandable, was created. It was also my desire to include resources with the book that would complement the material and make it easy for new entrepreneurs to understand the important tasks to be completed, and for established business owners to have a set of tools to help them grow their enterprise.

Working in a mentoring program assisting new and existing entrepreneurs with strategy planning is very gratifying work to me. Most business owners go it alone and don't get professional help. This is one of the reasons why so many businesses fail in the first few years. Strategizing reduces risk, thus improving the chance for success. I find it very rewarding to see new businesses reap the benefits of sound planning and becoming profitable. I want to thank several people for the opportunity I was given to participate in these programs. Jack and Judy Gregory managed the Community Business Access Center in Newmarket, Ontario and Cathy Greer established the Business Enterprise Resource Network in Barrie, Ontario. I was fortunate to work for a number of years as a mentor and consultant in both of these programs.

I would also like to mention several individuals for their assistance in verifying some of the resources presented in *The Small Business Planner* and for their input in several professional sections. Rychard Lardner of Lardner & Company, Chartered Accountants in Barrie, Ontario, provided feedback on many of the financial and planning templates and verified portions of the *Finance* section; Joanne McPhail, a corporate lawyer with the law firm Burger, Rowe in Barrie, Ontario, for providing input on some of the areas in the book covering legal considerations; and Cathy Wood, for her assistance in proofing and compiling the text. It can't be emphasized strongly enough, as outlined in Section 1, *Starting Your Own Business*, the importance of assembling a strong team, including professionals, to guide you in accounting and legal matters.

A companion web site for the book, www.consultbiz.net, has been developed to provide free resource templates and a forum for small business owners to share experiences and solve problems. Whether you are a seasoned entrepreneur, or starting a brand new enterprise, I am confident that the resources provided in *The Small Business Planner* will help you enjoy many years of self-employment success and self-gratification.

contents

list of figures and tables

introduction

Statistics don't lie and they all point to one conclusion – a majority of small businesses fail within the first five years. Of the businesses that do make it over this hurdle, many just get by and don't realize their full potential in growth or revenue for the owner(s). The big question here is – why? There may be several reasons why so many small businesses struggle and / or go under. Before we analyze the reasons, let's take a look at the basic business structure for a moment. To simplify things, all businesses large or small, product based or conceptual, service or manufacturing, have three main modules that interact. *Marketing* is covered in section two of this book, *Finance* in section three and *Operations* in section four. The strategies and action planning techniques discussed are based on North American business models, however, most of these concepts will work in almost any country in the world, as do the finance checks and balances. You will be introduced to a new *Marketing Planning Process* model that I developed to help business owners understand the importance of *First Things First* in creating an action plan. I will also be sharing a number of my own experiences from personal business dealings and those of others that I have witnessed as a consultant, instructor and mentor of new and seasoned entrepreneurs.

The first section, **Starting a New Business**, provides a list detailing the numerous tasks that must be addressed when starting a new enterprise. What it takes to be successful, conducting a feasibility study, building your team of professionals, legal and accounting considerations, along with selecting a business name and style are only a few of the many related topics discussed in detail. Available with the book are all the files you need to start you on your way. These include a *Profit & Loss, Cash Flow and Start-Up Cost* work sheets in

Microsoft Excel 97–2003, all customizable and complete with formulas. (See the Resource section at the end of the book for more details and a complete list of templates.)

The second section of the book covers the ***Marketing Module***. Finance deals with managing money properly for business growth and longevity. However, if you don't make sales, there is nothing to manage and that is where a sound marketing strategy comes in. Since this is the module where many small business owners fail miserably, it will be dealt with first. The most common reason for business failure next to poor financial management occurs in the development, or lack of development, of an effective marketing plan. It is common for new and even experienced entrepreneurs to let their guard down and become complacent when it comes to understanding customer's needs and positioning their offerings effectively against the competition. Assuming, or thinking you know your customer just doesn't cut it in today's competitive market which means you must do your homework and plan properly. Developing the *marketing message* without proper planning almost always results in wasted advertising dollars and inadequate sales.

The *Marketing* section of this book starts off describing the *Ten Most Common Marketing Mistakes*. It introduces the reader to the *Marketing Planning Process* model, and then goes into detail on the proper methods to develop a strategy that will position your company to make money. This is followed by chapters that cover the development and delivery of an action plan to make it work, including an in depth discussion of advertising tips and sales skills that many business owners will need. This module includes a template for a *Marketing Plan* in *MSWord 97–2003* format, a *Media Plan* and *Sales Call Sheets* in *Microsoft Excel 97-2003 file format* that can be downloaded from the book's companion web site, www.consultbiz.net. (M*ore details on the templates can be found on the Resources page at the back of the book.*)

The third section details the ***Finance Module*** which includes some of the most important functions in a business. Finance, in a basic sense, is simply about managing money, and failure to practice sound financial management is the most common and quickest way to create a business failure. When it comes to business finances, just like household finances, income or revenue must over time exceed expenses or the result eventually is bankruptcy. There must also be a way of measuring this in-flow and out-flow of money, and in businesses, the bookkeeping system does this to ensure compliance with government regulations. In addition, a good set of books and the timely reports they create provide management with a clear indicator of the company's financial health. This allows the initiation of appropriate controls if necessary to maintain profitability and growth. Extending credit comes with risks and this subject is covered in depth. This book includes access to templates for a *Business Plan* in *MSWord 97–2003* that is pre-formatted (requires the *Marketing Plan* insert – also included); a *Profit & Loss and Variance Analysis* work sheet in *Microsoft Excel 97–2003* that is customizable and complete with formulas.

The final section of the book discusses the **Operations Module**, which covers, as it describes, operational processes such as: facility, IT (Information Technology), supply, production, shipping and warehousing logistics, management, personnel, research and development and contingency planning. The chapters in this section will help entrepreneurs avoid making costly mistakes when it comes to developing effective web sites, employee relations, and contingency planning.

There is a tremendous amount of information available on the Internet. Due to the fact that web site addresses are constantly changing, very few were included as resources in this book. It is suggested that the reader conduct a search of their own on any given topic using their favorite search engine and a multitude of resources should be available.

If one idea from this book can help you to increase revenue or save money by avoiding common mistakes and pitfalls, then I have accomplished my goal. There is nothing more gratifying than operating a successful small business. This book should be of tremendous benefit to a new entrepreneur, many of whom jump into the turbulent world of business without testing the water or seeking outside professional advice. The seasoned business owner will also find this book of benefit as a reminder to keep pace with the rapidly changing business environment. Remember, there are only two criteria that must be satisfied for you to be a successful entrepreneur. First, you must love what you are doing and have a passion for it; and second, you must be able to pay yourself and make a profit.

THE ONLY BOOK YOU WILL NEED TO START AND OPERATE A PROFITABLE SMALL BUSINESS

Section 1:

starting your own business

Entrepreneurship can be one of the most gratifying life experiences available to the right individual. That's correct – the right individual. Successful entrepreneurs can be any gender; come from any socio-economic group; or, posses any level of education. There are certain qualities that are required, such as the 3 Ds of <u>D</u>iscipline, <u>D</u>rive, and a <u>D</u>esire to do whatever it takes to succeed. This eliminates a majority of the population, many of whom require the security of a regular pay day and prefer to have someone else tell them what to do. This section provides a check list of important tasks to complete when starting a new business and some insight into what it takes to give yourself a good chance to succeed.

1.1 Pros and Cons to Business Ownership

Figure 1-1   THE PROS AND CONS

PROS	CONS
• Being Your Own Boss	• Financial Risk
• Unlimited Earning Potential	• Possibility of Personal Failure
• Self-Esteem	• Solitude
• Tax Benefits	• Long Hours

Pros:

Being Your Own Boss – Do you get tired of taking orders and direction from someone else? If so, owning your own business may be the answer. Being your own boss is great incentive, but, are you really highest in the pecking order? An entrepreneur actually can have many bosses. They are all members of a group known as the business stakeholders. These include: lenders, who want to know you are managing their money wisely, shareholders who want to know you are managing their investment with sound judgment, employees who want to know they will have a job next week, suppliers who want to know you can pay your bills, and, probably most important of all, your customers, who want to know you will continue to provide the service and value they expect. How you deal with your bosses will have a direct bearing on your success.

Unlimited Earning Potential – In most cases when you work for someone else, you are on a fixed wage or salary. There is a ceiling on the amount of money you can make. As an entrepreneur, you set your aggressive, yet achievable goals and there really is no ceiling. Your incentive on one hand is a good income, yet on the other – poverty or going back to work for someone else.

Self-Esteem – There is no better way to improve self-esteem than to operate a successful business. It's great to start each day full of self-confidence and feeling good about yourself because you operate an enterprise that helps consumers or businesses with solutions that improve their life or profitability.

Tax Benefits – As a business owner, you will have many tax advantages not available to those individuals working for someone else. These tax breaks that you will discuss with your accountant include a number of ways to compensate yourself and numerous legitimate business expenses that can be written off.

Cons:

Financial Risk – Entrepreneurs must always deal with risk. Financial loss is the most obvious risk for a business owner who invests a great deal of personal money obtained from savings, mortgaging a home and personal guarantees for borrowed money from other sources. How you manage your finances and grow your business, especially in the first few years, will determine the success of the new venture. On the flip side, poor financial management generally results in business failure.

Possibility of Personal Failure – Closely associated with the risk of financial loss is the risk of personal failure. *"What if no one buys my product or service?"* This is a common thought of many new entrepreneurs. Risk is always a question mark looming over small business owners that can never be totally eliminated. It can be reduced by proper planning as described throughout this book. Many of the most successful entrepreneurs have bounced back from previous business losses and used the experience to grow stronger.

Solitude – This can be a "pro" for some people who like to work alone, but for most, the transition from a busy environment with co-workers and set business hours can be very difficult. A high level of self-discipline is required to stay on track and do what it takes to make it happen and achieve goals.

Long Hours – When the job needs to be done, most often in the early going, you are it! In the first few critical years of small business growth, the entrepreneur wears many hats. The skills necessary to wear each need to be learned and the appropriate number of hours must be dedicated to complete the functions required of the position. Although this period of growth requires long hours, it also requires excellent time management to block out the right amount of personal time for self and family.

1.2 Characteristics of a Successful Entrepreneur

Risk taker but not a gambler – One of the "cons" mentioned earlier was the risk of financial loss. In fact, there are numerous risks associated with entrepreneurship. If you are the type of person who must invest in guaranteed returns, think twice about starting your own business. With risk comes reward and entrepreneurs must be prepared to take advantage whenever the window of opportunity opens. But, don't jump in without testing the water first. Foolhardy gamblers can fall by the wayside quickly and painfully. There is no way to eliminate risk but there is a way to substantially reduce it – *Planning*. Proper planning, as described in this book, reduces the level of risk and improves your chances of success dramatically.

Making it happen – If you are not willing to make it happen then no one else will. This becomes most evident in new businesses that sell goods or services to other businesses, also referred to as a B2B enterprise, where the owner must cold call to obtain new customers. It is very easy to pick up the phone, but it is also very easy not to. The bottom line: if you don't pick it up and make it happen – there will be no revenue. This is where poverty becomes a powerful motivator.

Passionate about your idea – If you don't believe in what you are selling and if you don't feel passionately that you have a solution to satisfy your customer needs, then you should not be in that business. There are two ingredients necessary for success as an entrepreneur. You need to make money, of course, and you must have a passion for what you are doing. After all, one of the main reasons why people start their own business is because they hate their job!

Tenacious and persistent – These words describe the successful entrepreneur who must be prepared to take the good with the bad and never give up. In the early going there may be many lows when it comes to obtaining funding, getting customers, obtaining supplier credit, getting a good night's sleep, and the list goes on. An entrepreneur must be prepared to hear the word "no" and move on with optimism and enthusiasm. If you talk to enough people, someone is bound to say "yes" and buy your product or service.

Communication skills – When you own your own business, communicating effectively with other people is an absolute must. Customers, suppliers and employees form a short list of individuals requiring communication in all forms from verbal to written including print documents and Email messages. Your articulation in the languages you are using to carry on business will go a long way in showing your professionalism and being clearly understood.

Time management and organizational skills – Poor time management leads to wasted time and lost revenue. Stephen Covey's *"7 Habits of Highly Effective People"* is a good starting point to sharpen these skills. Without them, you will be continually putting out fires and dealing with urgent matters. Identify, prioritize and deal with important issues early before they become urgent and all consuming. Organize yourself and your office by using a day timer, contact management software or smart phone calendar and lay out your day and your week accordingly to maximize your time effectively. Be sure to develop a good filing system to retrieve and act upon important documents on demand.

People skills – An entrepreneur is always interacting with people and how you deal with stakeholders will have a considerable bearing on how smooth your business operates. Customers deserve and require exceptional service at all times and when you are fortunate enough to find good employees, they require excellent coaching, recognition when deserved, and incentives to keep them from checking the want ads for a better employer.

Access to capital – Most new businesses are drastically underfunded and this accounts in part for the high mortality rate in the first few years. New enterprises require sufficient start-up capital for asset procurement and operating costs including facility and renovating, initial supplier payments (you probably won't have credit yet), and marketing expenses. Don't forget to include enough funding to pay yourself a wage for the first three to six months as you get started. It will take some time to generate sufficient revenue and you still have personal commitments to meet.

1.3 Assessing Your Business Feasibility

You have a business idea and it involves doing something that you really enjoy. It may have been a hobby in the past, but your hard work and savings over the years have put you in a position to go out on your own, trying something you really have fun with. Congratulations! You have just satisfied the first part of the equation in becoming a successful entrepreneur. How about the second part – making a profit? Oh – forgot about that one! Most fledgling entrepreneurs do forget about this part and they jump in with both feet. Some do stay afloat – but most don't. Why? They didn't conduct any pre-planning to determine if their new business can actually be profitable. Prior to spending any money on your new business, do yourself a big favor and conduct a feasibility study. The results of this exercise will provide you with enough information to make an informed decision about moving forward. The study involves two parts: a *Market Attractiveness Study* and a *Financial Analysis*. *Figure 1-2* summarizes the requirements for each part of the study.

Market Attractiveness Study

In business planning, nothing can be assumed. If the market is not attractive for a new player, then you will struggle and most likely fail. A *Market Attractiveness Study* is conducted by looking at several important factors that include the number of accessible customers, competition, and market growth.

- *Accessible Customers:* How large is the market for your product or service and are the customers readily accessible? There should be enough customers available for you to obtain a market share that will sustain your business. Customer accessibility determines your cost to deliver the goods or services. Once you have an idea how large the market is, the number of people your company will be competing against must be determined.

- *Competition*: How many other businesses are providing the same product or service to the same market group? Of course, the smaller the number of players, the better it is for you. If you can take a totally unique idea to the market place, competition will not be a factor – at least in the early going.

- *Market Growth:* It may be something you always wanted to do, but if it is not an area of growth you will have a long uphill battle. Be sure to do your home work! Any business involving new technology, computer training and services for seniors are examples of growth markets. A special note here, if you are planning to start an Internet based business, the operating costs will be lower than a brick and mortar storefront. However, unless you are introducing something that no one else has thought of, the competition is likely to include thousands of other web enterprises. To succeed on the Internet you need a unique idea or delivery system. People generally purchase on-line because it is convenient and the price is lower.

These topics are covered in detail in the Marketing section.

Figure 1-2　FEASIBILITY STUDY

MARKET ATTRACTIVENESS	FINANCIAL ANALYSIS
• Potential Customers	• Profit & Loss Projection
• Accessibility to the Market	• Start-Up Costs
• Competition	• Available Capital
• Market Growth	

Financial Analysis

- *Profit and Loss Projection:* The most important tool in business for completing any kind of financial analysis is the spreadsheet. It is described in more detail in the *Financial* section. (*See Figure 3-3 for a sample P&L*). The *P&L Projection,* also known as an *Income Statement,* is a yearly projection covering the first three to five operating years. It will tell the new entrepreneur if the business can be profitable and the break-even point. Remember to be conservative with revenue figures and liberal with expenses to provide a cushion. A *Cash Flow Projection* for the same period should also be completed.

- *Determining Start-Up Costs:* There are substantial costs associated with starting a new business and they must be carefully researched and listed. These may include a facility and equipment, leasehold improvements, office furniture, supplies and equipment, computer hardware and software, initial cost of supply or inventory, vehicle, marketing collateral and advertising costs, professional fees, working capital and your own living expenses for three to six months of operation. (*See Figure 1-3*).

- *Capital Availability:* Once the complete list of start-up costs has been established, a determination can be made as to the amount of capital required to launch your new business. Subtract from this amount the money you can personally invest and you will know how much funding must be obtained from other sources such as loans and investors.

(*Profit & Loss, Cash Flow Projection and Start-Up Cost Analysis worksheets are available for download free with this book. These handy templates are fully formatted and ready to use in Excel 97-2003 file format. See the Resources section for more information.*)

Figure 1-3   START-UP COST ANALYSIS

Capital Costs			Sources of Start-Up Capital		
Land / Building Purchase	$		Owner Equity Investment	$	
Building Construction	$		Shareholder / Partner Investment	$	
Leasehold Improvements	$		Loan	$	
Mfg. / Production Equipment	$		Line of Credit	$	
Shipping / Warehousing Equipment	$		**Total Start-Up Capital Available**	**$**	-
Office Equipment	$				
Computer Hardware	$				
Computer Software	$		**Total Start-Up Costs**	**$**	-
Office Furniture	$				
Office Fixtures	$				
Retail Displays / Equipment	$		**Capital Surplus / (Deficit)**	**$**	-
Vehicle Purchases	$				
Vehicle Lease Deposits	$				
Total Start-Up Capital Purchases	**$**	-			

Start-Up Inventory		
Inventory	$	
Shipping	$	
Total Start-Up Inventory Costs	**$**	-

Operating Costs		
Office Supplies	$	
Marketing Collateral / Sales Tools	$	
Advertising	$	
Professional Fees	$	
Web Site Development	$	
Training	$	
Publications / Directories	$	
Insurance	$	
Other Expenses	$	
Deposit - Rent	$	
Deposit - Utilities	$	
Total Start-Up Operating Costs	**$**	-

TOTAL START-UP COSTS	**$**	-

Making the Decision

Now that you have completed your *Market Attractiveness* survey and a comprehensive *Financial Analysis*, it is time to make a determination on moving forward with your business idea. Keeping in mind the critical factors of making a profit, being competitive and having enough money to do it right, you will be faced with one of three decisions. You can move forward comfortable that all indicators are good and start developing a more comprehensive business plan and marketing strategy. It is then safer to start making the increased investment required. However, if it does not appear that your business can be profitable and competitive, you can either abandon the idea entirely and save yourself from a large financial loss, or, re-work the venture until it looks feasible. A special note here on starting an Internet based business. Many people are under the false assumption that it is easier to become successful with a web based business because the expenses are lower than those of a typical brick and mortar establishment. This couldn't be further from the truth. Sure, you won't have the rent, but you will have competition, and lots of it. Just conduct a search for the key words that will be critical to people finding your product or service. There will likely be millions of sites returned and thousands of other similar on-line businesses pitching the same idea. Money can be made on the Internet, but only if you have a unique product, service or delivery system. Many people think they can develop a web site and the traffic will come flooding in and this just doesn't happen. More on this topic in section 4.2, *Developing Effective Web Sites.*

1.4 Legal and Accounting Considerations

Assembling Your Team

Think you can go it alone? Many people try to do everything on their own and fail because they don't take advantage of professional help. There are many tasks involved in starting a new business and they all need to be completed properly. New entrepreneurs can't be expected to understand all aspects of business management. To fill the void, a team of experts must be assembled to ensure that you are making the right decisions in many critical areas. They may include a partner, lawyer, accountant, bookkeeper, banker, insurance broker, or a business consultant.

Partners – can bring a certain business expertise to your enterprise and they can also be a source of additional capital investment. This topic is discussed in more detail later in the *Partnership* business type section.

Legal – Once you have made the decision to move forward with your business idea, you should consult with a lawyer specializing in corporate matters. They will provide you with sound advice about registering your business, employment and labor law issues, liability considerations, name searches, intellectual property protection, and drafting partnership or shareholder agreements along with contracts if required.

Accountant – Every year you will be required to submit a tax return for yourself regardless of business type and a return for the company if the business is incorporated. A Chartered or Certified Accountant will find you the tax breaks and ensure that government regulations are adhered to. An accountant can give you advice on company type to register, setting up your books and the best way to write off business expenses. You will need to provide them with a good set of books at year end for the preparation of tax returns. A set of year ending adjustments will be returned to your bookkeeper to keep company financial records current.

Bookkeeper – Most new business owners don't have the knowledge to keep their own books, nor the time to learn. If this situation sounds familiar, hire a bookkeeper to set up your books based on your accountant's advice. Paid on an hourly basis, a freelance bookkeeper will keep your company books current, make government remittances as required, provide you with timely reports to measure and manage finances and give your accountant accurate year-end records. Whether you complete this important function yourself or hire someone else to do it, the only outcome that counts is that you are doing it – and doing it right! This is a critical element of business that must not be overlooked.

Banker – Your customers need a method to pay you and suppliers need to be paid. The heart of your business finances are found in the company bank account. Once you have registered your company, make arrangements to meet with a commercial account manager at your selected financial institute and set up the required accounts and privileges. Customers will want to use the easiest method possible to pay for your products or services. This may include checks, credit cards, bank card payments or credit. Your company will also need numerous suppliers that may provide any combination of raw materials, inventory, office supplies, advertising, printing, or vehicles. They may accept checks, credit cards, bank cards or offer you a credit account.

Insurance – An often overlooked member of a well chosen professional team is the insurance broker. There are many areas of operation that require protection to guaranty continuation in the event of a catastrophic or unforeseen event. This coverage may include business liability, comprehensive coverage for building and equipment loss, inventory losses, vehicles, key person insurance, owner's life insurance, owner's disability insurance along with error and omissions insurance (protection if sued). You should investigate the benefits of becoming a member of an industry association or a chamber of commerce as some of these plans may be offered at discounted group rates to members.

Consultant—Although there is no need to go it alone, most new entrepreneurs decide to take the lonely road and often end up making unnecessary mistakes that can end their dream abruptly. Assembling the right team of professionals and proper planning can eliminate much of the risk. Another professional you may want to consider for your team is a consultant. Some are specialists in areas such as marketing or IT and others are general business consultants. Knowledge in all areas of business management and operations is a prerequisite to success. If there is a grey area, consider hiring a consultant for advice or hands-on assistance with any part of your planning or delivery of action programs. Shop around and get references from their existing clients then take advantage of their experience and expertise. In lieu of hiring a consultant, take some business courses, read books and learn as much as you can about every business module – *Marketing*, *Finance* and *Operational* functions that apply to your business. You have already made a great start by reading this book.

1.5 Business Name and Registration Type

Give careful consideration to your enterprise name. At this stage of business startup, the biggest mistake is to rush out and register a name that sets you up for failure. Yes failure! That's how important your name is – I mean your business name – not your own. There is a tendency at this point for many people to use their family name. Understandable, since you likely haven't studied marketing and at this stage "*it's all about you*" – right? Unless you are a contractor or professional with a firm or a practice, try to avoid using your own name. Attempt to come up with a descriptive name that your customers will recognize easily as it relates to the products or services that you are selling. Try to come up with a name that will appear near the front of alpha directories, isn't long or confusing, and if possible, choose a name that is unique. You may want to hold off until you read the *Marketing* section of this book and start learning that "*it's all about the customer*" and <u>not</u> you!

It is strongly recommended that you seek professional legal advice before registering your new business. You will need to have a search conducted to ensure that you can use the new name legally without infringing on any trademarks. This type of intellectual property protection can be extremely valuable. When registered, a trademark claims rights over a name in relation to specific wares and services. There is a tremendous amount of information available about this subject on the Internet and it is possible in some cases to register trademarks yourself, with an agent, or a lawyer specializing in intellectual property. You should also discuss with a lawyer, the best way to legally operate and register your new enterprise. In some jurisdictions you can operate an enterprise simply in your own name and separate business expenses from personal income for tax purposes. However, it is highly recommended that you legally register the business and enjoy the benefits of using a proper business name with a dedicated bank account. Ask your lawyer if a sole proprietorship, partnership or incorporated business is the best way to proceed. Whichever way you decide, keep in mind that registering a business name simply advises the government about your identity and does not provide a legal right to use it exclusively. Only when you register a trademark is there a legal exclusion to others in the use of that name or style. The following is a brief description of each type of business entity.

Sole Proprietorship – is the simplest form of business registration.

- Easy set up and maintenance.
- Low cost registration.
- Business and owner are one-in-the-same.
- Owner is liable for all business activities.

Name searches and sole proprietor business registrations can be done on the spot at many State or Provincial government business service centers or on-line for a reasonable fee. The new owner can take the registration form to the bank and open a business account. In a sole proprietorship, all business activities are also those of the owner. The money the business takes in is that of the owner who must include it on their personal income tax return minus allowable business expenses. Accurate business records must be kept in accordance with sound bookkeeping practices even though the business itself is not taxed directly. Should you ever be selected for a tax audit, a good set of books will help government scrutinizers identify the legitimate company expenses and gain an appreciation for your business professionalism. If the business is sued – the owner is sued as well. If start-up capital is limited, you can register a sole proprietorship to save money and incorporate your business later if that style is preferred.

Partnership – is very similar to the sole proprietorship with the exception that two or more people jointly own the business.

- Partners bring additional start-up capital.

- Partners can bring expertise and experience lacking in some areas.

- Partnerships often end in broken friendships.

Partners have a similar role as the sole proprietor and share the risk. The exception to this rule is a limited partnership where certain individual liability is reduced or eliminated. In some jurisdictions, there are significant legal implications to operating a partnership, which should be discussed with a lawyer along with the partnership agreement. The primary reasons to take a partner into a business would be the input of additional capital or expertise in an area of administration or operations that is otherwise absent. Many partnerships fail because both individuals have similar skills and experience. If one has a production background and the other a sales background, harmony is more likely to endure. A partnership agreement is a must in case one partner fails to fulfill their obligations, dies or wishes to buy the other partner out. There should be exit mechanisms built into the agreement in the event that the partnership does not work out and the partners decide to go their separate ways.

Corporation – is the most expensive and complex business format to set up, however, it has many advantages that should be considered. The word company usually signifies that you are referring to a corporation. In addition to your own tax return, there is also a requirement that the incorporated company submit a return to one or more levels of government. Your tax accountant will look after year end returns from the set of books you provide. Your lawyer can register your corporation if you decide it is the right way to go and in some jurisdictions this can be done on-line.

- A corporation is an entity that can purchase and own property including land, vehicles, equipment and other businesses.

- It is owned by the shareholders.

- It is operated by the directors.

- Liability is limited.

- A corporation can sue or be sued.

- This form of business registration offers more expense write offs and greater flexibility in owner remuneration.

A corporation is owned by one or more shareholders. In a simple set up, you could be the only shareholder and issue yourself ten or one hundred shares for a nominal price. This may become the first deposit in your new business bank account. If you have a partner or investors, a certain percentage of shares can be issued depending upon their investment and level of ownership. As with a partnership, you should have a written shareholder agreement drafted by your lawyer if there are other owners. This can give you a first option to purchase their shares if they decide to leave or if they die, and an exit mechanism for a final division of corporate property in the event of a breakdown in relations between shareholders. The corporation's operations are managed by the directors and administered by the officers; president, vice president, treasurer and secretary. In a very simple single owner corporation you may be the only shareholder, sole director and the president. Speak with your accountant about assigning someone the title of treasurer for the purpose of having a second signature for the company bank account.

The corporation is an entity that can purchase land, buildings, vehicles, equipment, any type of property and even other companies. It can also sue and be sued. Essentially the shareholders are not subject to civil or criminal liability over the operations of the company. The director(s) may be liable for certain government remittances and incidents of gross negligence. You are always responsible for any personal guarantees made to lenders or suppliers.

1.6 Liability and Contracts

In business, as in life, it can be dangerous to make assumptions without doing your home work. More trivial law suits are clogging North American courts than ever before and you never know where or when a malicious customer or employee will show their wrath. You can't assume that one of these individuals won't cross your path. You can't assume that employees will never have an accident. In business you must always be prepared for the worst case scenario. If someone is successful in obtaining a judgment against you, everything you worked so hard for could be in jeopardy. This includes business and personal assets if you are not protected. There are many ways to protect your assets and depending on the volatility of your business type and industry, some or all of the fire walls available should be utilized. What is volatility in this sense? If you have a simple service business there is much less likelihood for cause to be sued than a business that sells prepared food, for instance. In the latter, a complaint of tainted food can occur at any time, whether legitimate or not. Some of the firewalls available include: incorporating, business liability insurance, errors and omissions insurance, worker's compensation insurance (regulatory requirement in many jurisdictions based on industry) and the assignment of personal assets – possibly to a spouse in high risk businesses. Discuss your options with a lawyer before setting up your layers of defense.

Contracts

There are many instances in business where a contract should be, or even worse, should have been considered. Contracts benefit both sides and ensure that price, responsibilities, expectations and time lines are met. You can create an agreement yourself, but if there is any doubt about structure or content, have your lawyer draft one properly. Here are some areas, activities and groups that warrant contracts:

- *Customers* – if you are a contractor, consultant, or designer to name a few.

- *Suppliers* – such as web development, sales agents or custom work.

- *Employees* – confidentiality, non-competition, job description or contract workers.

1.7 Regulatory Compliance

The onus is on the business owner to ensure regulatory compliance and remittance at all levels of government. Some of the most likely encountered regulations are listed below.

- *Federal* – personal and corporate tax returns, employee deductions, human and civil rights legislation, federal taxes collected, and import / export licenses and fees.

- *State / Provincial* – retail sales tax collection, worker's compensation premiums, labor and employment standards, health and safety compliance, hazardous or toxic substance handling, medical benefit payments, and certain types of business or industry licensing and certification.

- *Municipal* – realty and business taxes, facility zoning compliance, and local business licensing.

1.8 Employees

One of the greatest assets of any business is its employees. Finding, motivating and retaining good people requires skill and for many, a new way of thinking. If there is a requirement for employees in your new business, here are some important considerations:

- *Employment Standards* – your responsibility to know and follow. In addition to human rights considerations, this area may include employee licensing or certification to operate certain types of equipment or handle hazardous materials.

- *Health and Safety* – employees have a personal life, just like you. When they finish working for the day, their family expects them home, safe and sound. It is your responsibility to ensure that the workplace is a healthy and safe environment for your workforce. This includes air quality, safety equipment, first aid stations, emergency procedures and adequate training.

- *Contract Employees* – certain conditions must be met for an employee to be considered eligible for contract status. Many business owners use this method to avoid paying their share of benefits, payroll deductions and insurance. Use caution – do your homework – do it right. Get professional advice before you force a worker to make their own tax installments. If a worker is injured on the job and they were not paid as an employee with worker's compensation coverage, the ramifications for the employer may be very severe.

- *Motivation* – along with compensation and proper coaching are all areas that must be understood if you are to find and retain good employees. These people are hard to find and, "My way or the highway!" simply doesn't work anymore.

- *Job Descriptions* – should be written for each position leaving no doubt as to the employee's duties and the company's expectations.

- *Recruiting and Training* – learn how to recruit good employees and once they are on board, provide them with all of the tools and training necessary to ensure success.

This topic is covered in greater detail in Section 4.3 – Employee Relations.

1.9 What Plan Is Right For My Business?

The obvious answer – any plan is better than no plan! The truth is that most businesses don't engage in regular business planning, or any planning at all. Of the businesses that do plan, a majority fail to execute effectively for a number of reasons that will be discussed later. Business planning is a catch all phrase for any type of strategy development that will provide business owners with a blueprint to help their enterprise achieve realistic goals in growth and profitably. In fact there are a number of different types of plans that a business may adopt depending upon their unique situation. We will look at several of the most commonly used forms of planning, but first, let's examine a common thread for each.

For any type of plan to work effectively, it must be written for a specific purpose and audience. It must clearly state the company objective for writing the plan and the goals in quantifiable terms. There must also be a method of measuring the results in a certain time frame. In the business plan itself, the goals are generally stated in the profit and loss forecasts. These are measured at regular intervals with real numbers generated from sales and tracked through your accounting software. A stand alone marketing plan or a strategic plan will also have budgets and sales projections clearly stated. Finally, any plan must have an implementation schedule, or action plan, that assigns tasks with dates and individual responsibilities.

Depending upon the audience, your document should have a cover page, appendix for additional information and the written plan should be well structured with a table of contents indicating section and subsection numbers of the key areas along with page numbers for quick reference. Located near the front of the document, the most important, and the last section written, is the *Executive Summary*. This details all key points from each section in one or two pages and must capture the reader's interest. There are numerous tools and templates available on the Internet to assist you in planning for your business. Formatted planning templates in *MS Word 97-2003* file format are available with this book in addition to a *Profit & Loss* and *Cash Flow* worksheet in *MS Excel 97-2003* file format. See the *Resources* section for details. Now, let's examine three of the basic types of plans.

The **Business Plan** is management's financial blueprint that describes how the business will function and depicts its operational characteristics. The *BP* details how the business will be capitalized and managed. The *"reason for being"* as outlined in the *Mission* or *Vision* statement and the market opportunity should be clearly defined. The plan should be written by the business owner(s) or principles with outside assistance as needed. *Business Plans* are generally written for new businesses or operating divisions and enterprises looking to raise capital. The *BP* covers the three primary business modules of *Operations*, *Marketing* and *Finance*. The financial institutes offer templates and tools for business planning. These are very good on the numbers side but most of the tools available from this source fall extremely short in the development of a solid marketing strategy. There is no question that the numbers are important, but if you can't generate the revenue, they are meaningless. A solid *Marketing Strategy* should be developed as a **plan within** the *Business Plan* itself.

The **Marketing Plan** is an integral part of any form of strategic business planning, but it can also be a standalone plan with its own financials. *MPs* are a roadmap for launching a new product or service, increasing market share, establishing new markets for existing products or periodically reviewing changing market conditions. The marketing planning process should conform to a logical progression that, if followed, will result in action plans that are effective. If the proper progression is not followed, the result is often the creation of junk mail and ads that no one pays attention to. An effective *Marketing Strategy* must be developed based upon research and analysis of real market conditions such as the economy, opportunities and threats. *Target Market* profiling and *Competitive Analysis* are exercises used to develop tactics and messages that can be implemented to produce measurable results. *(These terms are covered in detail in the Marketing Sections 2.3 to 2.5.)*

The *Strategic Plan* is utilized by established businesses to review all processes and lay out both short and long-term direction by redefining the organization's mission and establishing realistic goals to produce achievable results. It is based upon a (**SWOT**) analysis of the company's internal **S**trengths and **W**eaknesses along with identification of the external environment **O**pportunities and **T**hreats. *(Processes of the Internal and External environment are discussed in Section 4.4 – Contingency Planning).* The process involves the establishment of key result areas, and then as in most plans, the development of an action plan for implementation and a means of measurement within a stated timeframe. The external environment, primarily customer needs and competition, are constantly changing and should be addressed at least yearly by developing a new Strategic Plan. Many companies are slow to change and get left behind by innovative and proactive competitors who are quickly adjusting to changing customer needs and market conditions.

Why Plans Fail

There are a number of reasons why plans fail. These include:

- Poorly defined strategies, or neglecting to state goals in quantifiable terms. It is easy to say, "We must increase sales." This goal is shallow without a stated amount and a time frame.

- The omission of clear implementation details.

- Lack of a management level commitment to change.

- The exclusion of employees where their *Buy In* is required for the successful execution of strategies.

No matter which form of planning you undertake for your business, the important point is that you are planning for growth and profitability. An informal plan may be sufficient for many small businesses, assuming that the proper strategy development has been completed. In the next section, the ground work for generating revenue by developing an effective marketing strategy will be presented along with an action plan to deliver impressive results.

There are many template variations and styles available for the different types of business related plans. There is no "right way" to prepare a plan – no rules written in stone. The key point is that you include enough information to answer any questions a reader may have and present it concisely with no spelling or major grammatical errors and in a manner where the information is easy to find. Remember, if you are in doubt about including a piece of information, go ahead and put it in. Supplemental facts and figures fit nicely into the *Appendix*. The templates available with *The Small Business Planner* do follow an order and layout that works very well. For the *Marketing Plan*, complete the sections before "*Action Planning*" first (except for the *Executive Summary*) as these sections clearly lay the ground work for your message and strategy. There are many resources available for planning. Go to the book's companion web site, www.consultbiz. net then click on the "*Links*" button for dozens of great planning sites.

Section 2:

marketing

Generating revenue and gaining customers for life.

2.1 Key Marketing Terms

Marketing is the actual managing of markets to bring about exchanges that satisfy needs and provide value. There are some terms in this definition that play a key role in understanding this process and require further explanation.

Market is a set of actual or potential buyers of a product or service. These buyers share a particular need that can be satisfied through exchange.

Needs represent a desire to fill a void – to obtain something that is lacking. *Needs* are satisfied with *Benefits* and people do not generally buy anything unless there is a need. Our job as marketers, is to determine who our customers are and what their <u>core</u> *needs* really are. Determining needs is detailed later in the *Marketing Planning Process* section. This is a good time to introduce a concept that will be repeated several times: "Your customer does not need what you are selling!" Yes, you heard right. But, your product or service <u>must</u> provide *Benefits* that satisfy the customer's need. It may sound a little confusing now but it should come together for you later in this section.

Value can be defined as the usefulness or importance of a product or service to the possessor. *Value* is always determined by the customer as a balance between price and quality. All marketers strive to provide value. Low price does not necessarily equate to value if the product is worthless to the customer or does not satisfy their needs.

Benefits are attributes of a product or service that satisfy core customer needs. They answer the question, "*What's in it for the customer?*" *Benefits* will sell products and services.

Features are often confused with benefits. Unlike benefits, features do not satisfy needs and do not sell a product or service. They simply differentiate a product or service from that of the competition and answer the question, "*Why should I buy from you?*"

Marketing Mix – The 4 Ps of the marketing strategy which are designed in to the mix of Product, Price, Place, and Promotion to develop effective tactics.

2.2 Ten Common Marketing Mistakes

Very few entrepreneurs seem to have a good understanding of marketing and the marketing planning process. When I ask small business owners what they think marketing means, most will say advertising, promotion, or sales. Although these activities all play an important role in the delivery of the action plan, they are not part of the research and development required to create the right message and strategy necessary for the delivery of a successful marketing plan. Doing it right helps business owners understand the dynamics of the exchange process and initiate tactics that will generate revenue. Given the importance of this aspect of business, it is surprising that so many entrepreneurs take their message to the marketplace without first doing their home work. The result is most often the creation of junk mail, ads that are ignored and a negligible return on advertising dollar. The following are some of the most common small business marketing mistakes that I have encountered. Each will be discussed in more detail later.

MISTAKES MADE BEFORE ACTION PLAN IMPLEMENTATION

Lack of Focus

Most new and many seasoned business owners assume that everyone is their customer. This is a very common problem with small businesses that don't want to lose a sale and the result is a diluted message that no one pays attention to. This mistake is overcome through target market analysis and market segmentation. This process will narrow the target market to ensure that the resulting message is focused. There may be more than one distinct market segment identified, and that is fine, provided that a different strategy and action plan is developed for each. You will find this topic discussed in more detail in *Section 2.4 – Target Marketing*.

Misunderstanding Customer Needs

The truth is that you sell entirely to needs and if you don't get this one right it will be very costly. If the need is not properly identified then people will not buy. Your customer does not necessarily need what you are selling, but your product or service must have a benefit that satisfies their need. If you don't have a clear understanding of your customer and their core needs then how can you possibly expect them to buy your products or services? To get this right, entrepreneurs must be able to look at the world through the customer's eyes instead of making assumptions that are incorrect by viewing the world from their own perspective. Due to the fact that market variables and needs change, this process should be repeated on a regular basis. This topic is also covered in *Sec. 2.4*.

Name

What's in a name? When it comes to marketing – everything! Very little thought goes into many business or brand names from a marketing viewpoint. One of the biggest mistakes involves the utilization of personal surnames as a business brand. This is commonly accepted practice for professional firms or contractors but it can be a tremendous roadblock for most other types of business. There is a huge cost associated with branding a name. Many names adopted by small businesses are confusing. Thought should also be given to the alphabetical positioning of your name in directories. Unless you've already paid the high price of making your name a household word, it should let people know what you do. If it doesn't, consider changing it, or attach a tag line to describe what you are all about. You will find this topic discussed in more detail in *Section 2.5.3 – Positioning*.

Lack of Competitive Intelligence

Unless you know your competition inside-out, an effective positioning and marketing strategy is impossible to develop. Learning who they are; where they are;

what their prices are; their strengths and weaknesses; how they reach the market; and how their customers perceive them, are key questions that must be answered to successfully differentiate you from the competition. This will also assist with your own pricing strategy and promotion effectiveness. You will find this topic discussed in more detail in *Section 2.5.1 – Competitive Advantage.*

MISTAKES MADE AFTER ACTION PLAN IMPLEMENTATION:

Poor Image

Image can be everything in marketing and a poor one creates a problem that is difficult and sometimes impossible to correct. How many chances do you get to create a good first impression? Think about that when you create your own logos, brochures, flyers, displays, web site or anything else that a potential customer will use to judge your professionalism and credibility. Lack of resources is often part of the problem here, so if you can't do it right, hold off until it can be produced professionally, even if it means completing the project in phases. A three page professionally designed and developed web site is better than an eight or twelve page site that looks home made. You will find this topic discussed in more detail in *Section 2.8.1 – Creating Effective Ads.*

Integrated Action Plans

Combining a single strategy and message for multiple market segments generally results in junk mail or ads that are confusing and ignored. If more than one market segment is identified, a different strategy and marketing mix (4 Ps - *product, price, place, promotion*) is required for each. This means a message for the secondary market that addresses different needs than those of the primary market. You will find this topic also covered in *Section 2.8.1 – Creating Effective Ads.*

Using Your Name as Headline

Again, unless it is a household word, using your name as a headline for your ads is one of the biggest and most common mistakes a small business can make. In actual fact, you are competing with thousands of other advertising messages that people are bombarded with every day. Branding has a high price tag attached to it. If the prospective customer cannot associate your name with a benefit, it will most likely get filtered out. Using a good headline or graphic illustrating the benefits is much more effective at getting their attention than using your own small business name – often done for the sake of vanity. This topic is discussed in *Section 2.8.1 – Creating Effective Ads.*

Poorly Developed Media & Sales Plans

Poorly developed strategies in this area most often results in wasted dollars spent on advertising media that have little chance of delivering results. If your business sells primarily to consumers (*B2C*), you should be concentrating your efforts on advertising – getting your strong message to the target market in the appropriate places. If your enterprise sells primarily to other businesses (*B2B*), then you should be focusing more of your attention and resources on creating effective sales tools and training with less emphasis on advertising. You will find this topic discussed in more detail in *Section 2.10 – The Marketing Budget and Media Plan.*

Poor Customer Service

This is the primary reason why customers switch to the competition. Retention strategies are often overlooked by companies of all sizes. It will cost you much more to bring a new customer on board than it will to up sell or retain an existing one. A satisfied customer is the best way to convince others to buy from you. What is the ten year reward in revenue from one good customer? A customer who is dissatisfied will not only starve you of this ten year revenue, but convince others to stay away. When is the last time you conducted a customer satisfaction survey? Information is power and this is where a good database and *CRM* (*Customer Relationship Management*) software is essential. You will find this topic discussed in more detail in *Section 2.12 – Customer Service.*

MARKETING RESEARCH - *Designing the Strategy*

2.3 The Marketing Planning Process

Having assisted hundreds of new and experienced entrepreneurs through the stages of business planning, I noticed one common thread. Almost all of them went into the marketplace with a message that was based on their own bias. "*It's all about me*" doesn't cut it in the real world of changing customer needs and intense competition for a limited market share. The importance of taking your time and creating an effective message based upon sound strategy development cannot be emphasized enough. This means understanding all aspects of your primary, secondary, and if applicable, tertiary markets along with a complete understanding of the competition. Once this preliminary research is completed and analyzed, an action plan with effective messages can be developed. These messages become the heart of all promotional efforts leaving only the task of determining where, when and how to deliver them.

A plan is similar to a roadmap. It is meant to take you from a starting point to a specific destination by the most effective route. When planning a trip, people lay out the route they are going to take from start to finish. When planning for a business, why would anyone try to jump in at the middle of a route intended for marketing success without doing their research? The answer is simple – most entrepreneurs do not have formal marketing training and really don't know where to start. To make the process clear for the purpose of marketing planning, I created a model which is actually a time line showing the stages in the *Marketing Planning Process*. Taking a look at *Figure 2.1*, most small business owners tend to jump right into the action plan stage with advertising messages that haven't been developed by sound research techniques and most often prove to be ineffective and costly. The model prompts people to follow the time line in completing planning objectives in order to create a message that is more effective in generating revenue. The *Marketing Plan* template in *MS Word* available with this publication is also set up in accordance with the model to help users complete the tasks in the proper order.

All areas on the time line to the left of the vertical dividing line must be completed prior to moving forward with the *Action Plan*. In the *Marketing Plan* template, there are a number of sections that are to be completed before action planning, however, the two critical areas with the greatest impact on the message are the focus of the model and our discussion. *Target Marketing* involves research in determining market size and understanding customer needs. This answers the important question, "***What's in it for the customer?***" A thorough analysis of the competition's strengths and weaknesses along with a clear understanding of all aspects of their business conduct allows you to position your business and answer the question, "***Why should I buy from you?***"

- *Primary Research* – is conducted by you or a marketing company hired to conduct surveys, establish test markets or facilitate focus groups.

- *Secondary research* – has been conducted and published by someone else. Often this information is available over the Internet or from a library at no charge. Government census reports provide an amazing amount of demographic information on the population, most at no charge. Research companies charge for their reports unless you can get the information when it is first published in magazines or newspapers.

Figure 2-1   THE MARKETING PLANNING PROCESS

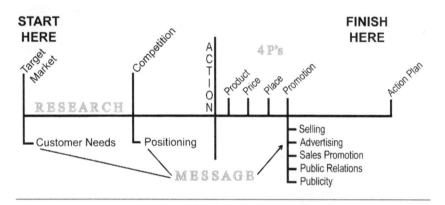

*Figure 2-1 is the **Marketing Planning Process** model that I developed to assist business owners in following tasks in a logical sequence to produce optimal results. The key areas left of the **Action** vertical line must be completed before delivering any promotional messages. Unfortunately, many business owners start on the right side of the Action line and develop a message that will be ignored.*

2.4 Target Marketing – Understanding Customer Needs

The first common marketing mistake discussed earlier is lack of focus. You've seen the cluttered ads where a business tries to mention absolutely every product or service they can offer for every type of customer imaginable. Most small businesses don't want to lose a sale, so they cram as much as possible into a tiny ad or make a flyer look like a dog's breakfast. The truth is, unless you sell bread, everyone is <u>not</u> your customer. Lack of focus can be a real killer because you end up throwing valuable advertising dollars out the window. Even when you do it right, it is still hard to compete against all of the other messages that consumers are trying to filter out. Making a mistake here is very costly in many ways; poor branding, higher cost to reach a broader market, lower return on advertising dollar, and lower sales, just to mention a few.

So, what's the answer? *Target Marketing!* Part of the preliminary marketing strategy development involves the creation of a *Mission Statement*. In developing this important statement from a marketing perspective, I like to ask several key questions, which if answered correctly, help us to focus. The first question deals directly with the target market when we answer, "*Who is my customer?*" The second question that requires an answer for the mission statement asks the question, "*What does the customer really need?*" The third deals with the way we satisfy those needs and conduct our business.

2.4.1 Market Segmentation

Back to the first question, it sounds pretty easy – "*Who is my customer?*" Although it may sound simple, this is actually a difficult question to answer, because most small businesses don't want to let go of a potential sale, and the answer is too often, "Everybody!" Many businesses have two or more market segments they sell to, and that is fine, but each segment will have a different profile and unique needs to satisfy. Therefore, each require their own message and action plan. First of all, a profile is created for each market group using demographic and psychographic target market segmentation.

- *Demographics* – categorizes groups of customers with similar buying characteristics using education; age; gender; marital status; occupation; income; religion; and race as criteria for segmentation. If you are an operation that sells to businesses, you will segment your markets using criteria such as industry type, geographic location, and business size based on annual sales or number of employees.

- *Psychographics* – categorizes groups of customers with similar buying characteristics using their lifestyles, hobbies and interests as criteria for segmentation.

Once your customers have been defined for the products or services being offered, they can be classified into buying groups, or target markets:

- *Primary Market* – This defined group is most likely to buy your product or service. They are the easiest group to deliver effective messages to and most of your promotional resources will be directed here. Your return on advertising dollar will be highest if the plan is executed properly with a focus on this lucrative market.

- *Secondary Market* – They require more effort and expense to initiate a sale. Your budget will not include a substantial amount to attract this segment as your return on advertising dollar is reduced, but they cannot be overlooked.

- *Tertiary Markets* – This group will buy on a small scale and little or no promotional resources should be allocated in attracting them as your return on advertising dollar will be negligible.

- *Invisible Customers* – They will occasionally purchase your offering but you are not really sure who they are or what group they fit in to. You certainly will not turn them away but no resources will be expended attracting this phantom group.

Demographic segmentation can substantially narrow each target market. Once the identified characteristics have been applied, the market size, market potential and sales potential can be determined. These statistics are available from federal agencies such as the Census Bureau http://www.census.gov in the United States or Stats Canada http://www.statscan.ca. They are also available from many local municipalities. Psychographic analysis gives us an indication about activities your target market likes to participate in. Where do they play? You now have a better idea how to reach the intended audience. Media demographics can be matched to your defined target audience demographics. Most television and radio networks, magazines and newspapers have audited statistics on their viewers, listeners and readers that you can match to your target audience. Apply this technique to each one of your target markets, but remember that each one requires a unique message as they are different people with different needs. Do not try to reach both groups at once and your ads will start to have more impact as they are not cluttered with several messages for different groups on a quarter page. The target audience must identify immediately with the message otherwise it will be blocked out like a majority of the advertising noise that people constantly filter out to maintain sanity. Go to the book's companion web site at www.consultbiz.net to access many valuable on-line resource links.

What Does The Customer Really Need?

Your ability to answer correctly will determine how effectively your message grabs the customer's attention. This is a very common mistake with small business and it involves the misinterpretation of customer needs. If the need is not defined properly then people are unlikely to buy – plain and simple. In order to develop an effective marketing strategy and create an attention grabbing message for a headline, the second question of the mission statement must be answered correctly. What does the customer need? It sounds easy – they need what I am selling….right? Wrong! This is a difficult question for business owners to answer but getting it right has a major impact on how well your message works in both advertising and personal selling because it answers the all important, *"What's in it for the customer?"*

It is human nature to look at the world through our own eyes and make assumptions. Unfortunately, when it comes to marketing, making assumptions about core customer needs based upon your own thoughts and observations often results in the creation of media campaigns that provide a zero return on advertising dollar and fill recycling bins with junk mail. Although it is difficult to do, the first step in correcting this problem, and worth repeating, is to admit that the customer doesn't really need what you are selling. However, the product or service you are offering <u>must</u> have a benefit that satisfies their core need. In order to get this answer right, it is imperative to look at the world through the customer's eyes.

Put yourself in your customer's shoes, look back at your business and answer the question, *"What are you really selling?"* For example, if you are an interior decorator, what does your customer really need? What are you selling? In this case the customer doesn't need an interior decorator – their core need may be a unique look that reflects their personality. The service offered has a benefit that satisfies that need. Now we can design a headline that is powerful in getting the attention of this market. If your product or service is targeted toward the more affluent then you may be selling bragging rights and some retailers may actually be selling a lifestyle and not a product. It is now possible to create a headline that will catch the attention of this target audience alone. The message is not meant for any other group as it will be ignored, and that is fine.

Let's try a *Business to Business (B2B)* example. What is a human resources consultant selling? The core need for a business customer is, of course, bottom-line profitability, but that is too general. Looking through the customer's eyes in this case, the need may be to have motivated employees who are more productive; a lower turnover rate as there is a high cost to recruiting and training; or just meeting legislated requirements and staying out of court. Strong benefit words can now be created for effective selling that will grab a prospect's attention and cause them to take a course of action that is favorable to your business. Customer needs can change and most certainly the external business environment is constantly changing. That is why it is important to re-visit your mission statement at least yearly answering the questions; "*Who is my customer?*" and "*What do they need?*" This keeps you thinking like a marketer and looking at the world through the customer's eyes instead of your own.

2.4.2 Surveys ✓

Determining customer core needs is often a difficult task. It may appear obvious for some types of businesses; however, for most it requires much consideration to arrive at the right answer. One technique that works very well is to brainstorm. Be sure to invite your front-line employees to join in brainstorming sessions as they are in close contact with the customers and should know them best. If you are starting a new business, try meeting with friends or associates who may be potential customers. In these sessions, all suggestions are good in creating a profile of the perfect customer along with their core needs and all ideas should get written down and posted for consideration. When these ideas are reviewed and a short list created, the assumptions you initially made can now be verified using sound methodology. This verification can be accomplished through primary marketing research in the form of a survey.

This survey can be formal—conducted by a marketing company or by you, using a set of pre-determined questions intended to define as well as confirm the customer profile and core needs. It can also include questions about their intention to buy and agreement or disagreement with product or service pricing. Surveys can be delivered by mail or the Internet but prepare yourself for a low return without the proper incentive. The accuracy of surveys returned by this method may be low along with the cost in comparison with other methods of delivery. Surveys can be conducted by telephone with increased accuracy or in person with the highest level of accuracy as you can see and hear the person and their responses. It is important to analyze a large enough sample to make an accurate determination of results.

The survey can also be informal, that is, a general discussion with members of the target market. In this case, the same objective questions must be used for everyone and the results accurately recorded for future analysis. Later, customer retention will depend on feedback usually received through satisfaction surveys. It is beyond the scope of this publication to go in to detail on survey preparation. There are many books available along with numerous resources on the Internet that can assist in the preparation and delivery of quality surveys.

You should now have a profile of the perfect customer along with a good understanding of their core needs. The answer to the first question of the message: "*What's in it for the Customer?*" can now be incorporated into your strategy.

2.5 Positioning

2.5.1 Establishing the Competitive Advantage

You have done a great job analyzing your target market, focusing, then determining customer needs. The first half of the message is answered solidly addressing these core needs with benefits and the customer has been convinced to make a purchase to fill the void. But something went wrong and they bought from your competitor. What happened here is a common mistake that many entrepreneurs make in not conducting a thorough analysis of the competition to answer the second question, "*Why should I buy from you?*"

In order to position yourself and convince the customer to buy from you, it is imperative that you understand your direct competition inside and out. Direct competition is defined as those businesses that sell the same goods or services to the same target market in the same geographic area. What should you know about the competition? The answer would be *everything possible!* Most large companies that manufacture consumer goods have a marketing department. Often within this department are individuals whose sole responsibility is the collection of competitive intelligence. This is such an important part of business today because without this valuable information it is impossible to effectively develop a positioning strategy. More on that later, but for now let's just look at answering this important question, "*Why should the customer buy from you?*"

The answer to this question forms the body of the message. Once you have the attention of the target audience by correctly answering the first question, *What's in it for the customer?*, it is necessary to let them know what features make you different. It is also important here to understand the difference between features and benefits. *Benefits* sell because they satisfy needs and if there is no customer need identified they won't buy. *Features* differentiate you from the competition, often measured by comparing price, quality or service. Before you can state exactly what your competitive advantage is, it is necessary to know, at a minimum, the following information about your competitors.

- First, identify who the direct competitors are and where they are located.

- Some investigating and research is required to learn how they reach their market. This information can help in the preparation of the promotion or media plan. A competitor who is established and enjoys a reasonably good market share must be doing something right. Why not copy some of these methods to reach your market instead of re-inventing the wheel?

- Examine competitive offerings and learn everything you possibly can about the quality and service. There are many ways to accomplish this including making actual purchases yourself and studying their web site or marketing collateral.

- Learn their pricing structure. Most businesses adopt a, *meet the competition*, pricing strategy. If you don't know what all direct competitor's charge then it is impossible to establish this type of pricing strategy effectively.

- How is the competitor perceived by their customers? This information is not as difficult to obtain as it may appear on the surface. Customers are often very willing to tell about their experience both good and bad. You need to know what they like about the competitor so the same level of service can be provided. You also need to know what they don't like about the competitor or what improvements the customer would like to see. The answers obtained here will definitely help you in the development of an offering that will clearly show your competitive advantage.

Figure 2-2   COMPETITIVE ANALYSIS WORKSHEET

Company	Promotion	Price	Strengths	Weaknesses
Competitor 1 Contact Info				
Competitor 2 Contact Info				
Competitor 3 Contact Info				

Figure 2-2 is the tool that will guide you through the competitive analysis process necessary to position yourself in the market effectively. In the first column list each direct competitor by name, address, phone number, key contact name and web site address if applicable. In the second column, list the methods they use to promote their products or services and collect any marketing collateral or ad copy available. The third column details their pricing. Having analyzed each competitor thoroughly, list the strengths that you will attempt to match and the weaknesses that you will plan to leverage and avoid making yourself. This table is available from the companion web site in an MS Excel 97-2003 worksheet. It includes extra columns for market share and a description of your own unique advantage. See the Resources section for more information.

2.5.2 Methods of Collecting Competitive Information

- Competitor's marketing collateral (flyers, brochures, catalogues) that can be obtained directly, usually from their web site.

- Personal observations made by visiting their showroom, speaking with principles or employees, observing the customers and suppliers who come and go from the premises.

- Analyzing competitive products and packaging by purchasing and using them.

- Speaking with some of their customers and suppliers to determine what is liked and disliked about the way the competitor carries on business.

The most important issue here is the fact that you have acquired the necessary information to correctly position yourself for market share and not so much how you acquire it. Of course it is always best to follow ethical and moral practices, yet if you or an associate are unable to call a competitor posing as a customer for the purpose of obtaining information, it could mean the difference between struggling and doing well.

Another important myth to dispel is the one where people think that the competition is bad. In fact, competition is good – for the consumer and for you. Much can be learned from competitors (*what to do and what not to do*) and some may be approachable enough to share some of their experiences. If a good business relationship has developed between you and your competitors, there may be sub-contract work or referrals if they are too busy, and vice versa. But always remember, they are still the competition so never drop your guard.

2.5.3 Positioning

Positioning is the place your product or service holds in the customer's mind when comparing your attributes to those of the competition. *Positioning* is all about differentiation and standing out for the right reasons.Armed with the wealth of information obtained from the competitive analysis, it is now possible to examine ways to differentiate your business. *Features* are the attributes used to differentiate – primarily using price, quality and service.

- *Price* is the most obvious feature that a customer can see to compare one offering to another. Is it a good idea to try to persuade customers to buy because you are the lowest price? Use caution with this one! People often associate low quality with low price. There is also the issue of profit. You must understand your margins and the effect of price change on your bottom line. More on this later.

- *Quality* is a good feature but a difficult one to use in the message for differentiation because you must prove what you say. You can't simply say, "*The customer should buy from us because we are better!*" If you can find an area of quality where you stand alone then by all means play it up in your message. If your product or service has a more environmentally friendly aspect then definitely let the customer know. Remember – it is not wise to say bad things about the competition. Customers appreciate hearing about pros and strengths and do not tolerate negative messages about others.

- *Service* is the area where you can often find a way to stand out. There are many aspects to service including: pick-up and delivery; return and exchange policy; warranties; customer reward programs; making it easier to do business; or just being more friendly and providing superior customer service, to name a few. But, keep in mind that there is a cost attached to many of these services so be prepared to factor in the added direct costs to determine profitability.

The bottom line here is providing more *Value* than anyone else. What is value? It is something perceived by the customer and it can be very different from person to person. *Value* can be a measurement of the benefit or enjoyment derived from a product or service at varying price levels. In a market with many competitors it can be almost impossible to differentiate and gain a satisfactory share. One of the best ways to differentiate your business from the competition is to find a way to become unique. If there is no other business providing the same product or service to the target market, you will be positioned alone – a great scenario until a new player decides to jump in to the race and copy you. If you are up against a large established competitor that commands a large market share, find a way to specialize. Dissect the offering to the target market and specialize in one area. This is known as *Niche Marketing* and it can be extremely effective in differentiating yourself in a highly competitive environment. In developing a positioning strategy it is important to emphasize and build your uniqueness into the *4 Ps (Marketing Mix),* product, price, place and promotion to be discussed later.

Now you are ready to move forward and develop the strategy that will go into the *4 Ps* of the action plan.

2.5.4 Marketing Strategy

Marketing Strategy describes how the information gathered from the target market and competitive analysis will be incorporated into the action plan through the mix to achieve company objectives. You now have enough information to create your marketing message and provide direct answers to the key questions:

What's in it for the Customer?

and

Why should I buy from you?

These answers will form the back bone of promotional activities to convince prospective target customers to buy from you. This will create your branding and image or how the customer will perceive you. Now, how about your name? If you have chosen a company name that is not descriptive of the benefits offered then a tremendous advantage has been lost, especially if you have chosen your family name for the business like mine, which is at the end of the alphabet. There is a solution. Either change your name or adopt a tag line. A tag line is a slogan of a few words that accompanies your business name everywhere. The tag line should consist of power words that describe the competitive advantage or a core benefit and it is meant to catch the customer's attention and help develop branding. The following lists some examples of places where your power words and tag line should appear.

- Attached to your name at all times to develop branding.
- On all company signage including vehicles.
- On your web site.
- In all advertising.
- On all marketing collateral.
- In your networking speech.
- In any scripts used for personal selling.

See if you can recall who some of these well known marketing tag lines belong to.

1- Takes a lickin' and keeps on tickin'; 2-Just do it!; 3-Where's the beef?; 4-Let your fingers do the walking; 5-Finger lickin' good; 6-The uncola; 7-The quicker picker upper; 8-Because I'm worth it; 9-How do you spell relief?; 10-Like a rock; 11-Nothing runs like a Deere; 12-Think outside the box; 13-Drivers wanted; 14-The king of beers; 15-Share moments – share life.

Tag lines can position you against – or away from the competition. Look at the tag line adopted by 7-Up and guess who they <u>do not</u> want to be compared to or positioned against!

ANSWERS: 1. Timex; 2. Nike; 3. Wendy's; 4. Yellow Pages; 5. Kentucky Fried Chicken; 6. 7-Up; 7. Bounty; 8. L'Oreal; 9. Rolaids; 10. Chevy trucks; 11. John Deer; 12. Apple Computer; 13. Volkswagen; 14. Budweiser; 15. Kodak.

ACTION PLANNING – *Implementing the Strategy*

The first set of common marketing mistakes discussed at the start of this chapter occurred during the strategy development process prior to action plan implementation. The remainder of the mistakes that were mentioned occur in the development and execution of the action plan – those tactics that make the strategy work. The illustration made by the *Marketing Planning Process* model *(Fig. 2-1)* clearly shows the tasks to be performed before action planning. Most companies ignore this area of planning and jump right to the *Action Plan* stage; printing flyers, brochures, and paying for print ads that will become trash or just ignored. This is most often a result of inadequate research and investigation to properly answer the key questions: *"Who is my customer and what do they really need?"* along with, *"Why should the customer buy from me?"* When developed properly, the marketing strategy developed can be built into the mix; the actual *Product*, the *Price, Place* (distribution to the end user), and *Promotion*. Let's examine the first three.

2.6 Product, Price, Place

- **Product**: This could include the actual product design, the packaging to reflect and restate your positioning, or a service business that clearly shows in the offering *"What's in it for the customer?"*, along with your positioning statement confirming the competitive advantage.

- **Price**: The offering must deliver value to the customer but you still need to make a profit. A critical mistake many businesses make with price is to position their product or service on low price. A low price strategy may work, if the bottom line <u>can</u> support it. You will know what these critical figures are from the *Profit and Loss* projection you created earlier. This is the minimum price you need to charge in order to sustain and grow your business. Beating the competition on price requires lower overheads (*fixed costs*); purchasing in higher volumes to encourage supplier discounts (raw material and resale products); or better economies of scale relating to manufacturing. If this isn't possible, try providing a better product or superior customer service. Some people don't buy a lower priced product or service because they often equate price with quality. The pricing strategy utilized by most small businesses is *Meet the Competition.*

Once you have set a price – stick to it! Print rate sheets and offer discounts on a consistent basis for volume purchases or quick payment only. Altering from your price sheet indiscriminately will result in a lack of credibility.

- *Place*: Refers to the way in which products will reach the end user. You may need to consider channels and develop channel partners from manufacturer, to wholesaler, distributor, dealer or retailer. Location can have a very large monetary effect on distribution and if you are an Internet business these issues primarily concern shipping to customers. If the plan is to develop a dealer network, a suggested retail price must be established for the product. This allows you to sell directly to the end customer without competing with your dealers, but, your retail price must always be the suggested list price and never lower.

PROMOTION

There are five ways to promote a business:

- Advertising
- Personal Selling
- Sales Promotion
- Public Relations
- Publicity

Advertising tops the list if you are a *B2C* (Business to Consumer enterprise) and all of the other methods are way down the list. This means establishing a budget that will cover advertising production and placement costs that will be outlined in the *Media Plan*. If you operate a *B2B* (Business to Business) then the primary way to promote your company is through personal selling, either a sales force or by you, the owner. This means your budget will be primarily for the development of effective sales tools. Other methods of promoting a business are *Sales Promotion*, *Publicity* and *Public Relations*. Although any one of these areas can achieve results if delivered effectively, the return in sales is minimal in comparison to the results that can be obtained from the primary methods of promotion listed for each type of marketing environment. (*See Fig. 2.3*)

2.7 Sales Promotion, Publicity and Public Relations

Although these methods of promoting a business are less effective than *Advertising* if you are *B2C* or *Personal Selling* if you are *B2B*, they are worth keeping in mind as part of your action plan. Let's take a look at them first before analyzing the primary methods of promotion. These methods are intended to bring recognition to your operation more than anything else. Except for publicity, there is a cost attached to effectively utilize each one of these secondary techniques.

Figure 2-3   PRIMARY METHODS OF PROMOTING A BUSINESS

Business to Consumer (B2C)	Rank	Business to Business (B2B)
Advertising	1	Personal Selling
Sales Promotion	2	Public Relations
Publicity	3	Sales Promotion
Public Relations	4	Advertising
Personal Selling	5	Publicity

As illustrated in Figure 2-3, if you are selling products or services to consumers, the primary method for promoting your business is advertising and everything else is far down the list for effectiveness and return. If your company sells products or services to other businesses, then personal selling tops the list.

Sales Promotion

There are two forms of sales promotion, both of which offer your target customer or your dealer incentives to purchase products from you. There is a cost attached to this form of promotion.

Consumer Promotion:

- *Free Samples* included with the primary product.
- *Coupons* for redemption.

- *Rebates.*

- *Patronage Rewards* with a point accumulation on purchases that can be redeemed at a later date for your products, or, bonuses such as dining or travel.

- *Contests* are also a form of sales promotion and a great way to build qualified prospects in the marketing database.

Trade Promotion:

- *Discounts.*

- *Promotional* products. (Items with your logo and branding).

- *Rewards* for achieving a set sales volume.

- *Co-Operative Advertising* with a dealer or retailer.

- *Trade Show* expenses.

Publicity

The only cost here is your time. Publicity is simply getting your name in front of people and there are several ways to accomplish this.

- Press Releases can be developed on newsworthy items about your business such as a new product launch, store opening or event sponsorship. There are basically two ways to get your word out via press releases. The first is to have an editor of a newspaper or magazine publish it, however, given the number of releases they receive each day it may need to be a *slow news day.* The other method is to send the release to all of your customers or prospects in your database and post it on your company web site. When drafting a press release, be sure to write it objectively like a newspaper article in the third person with a catchy but brief headline. It should also have a date for release and contact information including name, phone number, and Email address. (*See Fig. 2-4*)

- Public Speaking is a great way to gain an audience and expand your network. Many organizations, such as chambers of commerce and trade groups invite industry experts to address their members.

- *Publishing* articles and books is another way of spreading the word about you and your business. Many publications look for experts in various fields to write articles of interest for their readers. In return, a free ad and exposure is offered for the contribution, but try not to blow your own horn too much. The article is meant to help educate or entertain the reader in some way. A plug for your business is usually allowed at the end which should always include your web site address and contact information.

Figure 2-4   **SAMPLE PRESS RELEASE**

FOR IMMEDIATE RELEASE

DATE: March 4, 2011

CONTACT: Jennifer Smith

PHONE: (416) 222-1212

E-MAIL: jsmith@mycompany.com

YOUR ATTENTION GRABBING HEADLINE

TORONTO, ON.

Jennifer Smith, president of "My Company", announced ....

Body copy should be written objectively in newspaper style and in the third person clearly describing the event. Several brief and concise paragraphs should convey excitement keeping the size to one page in total length.

For more information check www.mycompany.com or

Call J. Smith at (416) 222-1212.

- End -

Public Relations

Public Relations is all about image and the way your company is perceived in the public eye. There is a cost attached to these activities which can often be a co-operative effort with another company, group or charity.

- *Charitable Donations* are guaranteed to create favorable opinion and this type of *P.R.* generally involves donating a percentage of sales for one day or another specified period of time to a popular charity. The event can often be promoted free as a community event by the sponsor along with local newspapers or radio stations.

- *Give-aways* such as providing items for the needy and sponsoring food drives can be effective. Providing product for high profile news-making events proved invaluable for Oakley Sunglasses during the *Miner Miracle* on October 13th, 2010. They supplied a pair of their glasses to each of the thirty-three miners rescued from the San Jose mine in Chile. You can't put a price on this kind of exposure where your product is viewed by millions of people on all major television networks worldwide.

- *Sponsorships* are another great way of getting your name in front of the public. Sponsoring local sports teams such as minor baseball, soccer or hockey provides youth organizations with the funds needed to operate league play and your name is front and center on the uniforms. If you provide sponsorship money for an event then be sure to get a plug for your business on the programs or advertising whenever possible.

2.8 Advertising

Even if you have developed a great message for each target market, there still remains a tremendous hurdle. People, namely your target audience, are bombarded with advertising messages every waking hour. Think about it! Radio, television, Internet, billboards, street benches, buses, taxis, magazines, newspapers, signs, displays and direct mail are all competing for their attention. There is no escape – so how do people maintain their sanity in light of this constant barrage of noise? They filter it out. The job of a good marketer is to generate a message that will break through this barrier and create some form of recall or action – ultimately the purchase of your product or service. Considering the daily competition marketers are facing, the message must be better, or it won't work, resulting in wasted time and money.

One way to break through the filters is to send a highly repetitive message over the air waves (*at a substantial cost*), until their will is broken. Some ads get attention by insulting the intelligence of the audience. This risky method does work in some cases as the individual recalls the product (possibly with some distaste), however, most small businesses do not have a budget for this kind of psychological warfare. The proper and economical way for most companies to create recall is by creating a headline for an ad or flyer, possibly in combination with a striking graphic, which has a good chance of catching the attention of the target audience. This message comes from the strategy development phase where customer core needs were established and verified. The headline should leave no doubt as to their identity, and when the target audience sees it, they will know it is directed at them alone. According to the popular marketing model AIDA, when you have their **A**ttention, grab their **I**nterest in your offering by showing how it will provide a solution and how you are different from everyone else. The next stage is their **D**esire to fill the void you have established in their mind (*core need*) which leads to the execution of your call for **A**ction – generally purchasing the product or service.

How many people read junk mail? You have approximately two seconds to catch your prospective customer's attention before your masterpiece lands in the trash which is where most of these messages end up. The same applies to poorly written ads in magazines and newspapers that readers skip over. Getting the attention of your target audience is the master key to successful advertising so if you're not sure about doing it right, hire a professional to help.

In many cases, individuals need to get emotionally charged before they buy. This can be achieved by using power benefit words in your headline. Remember, benefits satisfy needs and if these needs are not addressed then people won't buy. Attention can also be achieved by creating emotion using sympathy, fear, humor, or sex appeal often in conjunction with an eye catching graphic.

Many of the common marketing mistakes discussed earlier in this book occur at this stage of the plan.

2.8.1 Creating Effective Ads

Image Is Everything

The first of these mistakes is *image*, or should I say the wrong image and, it is worth repeating that you only get <u>one</u> chance to make a good first impression. This first impression is very difficult to change in people's minds if it is not favorable. Unfortunately many small businesses cut corners here. Instead of having a professional create an outstanding image, expenses are trimmed and key marketing collateral are created with inappropriate software and sub-standard creative ability resulting in the kind of branding that should be avoided. Company logos, brochures, flyers, print ads and the company web site all convey an impression to the target audience. Should you decide to tackle this important aspect of production yourself, make sure that you have the proper tools, the required level of skill, <u>and</u> the time to do it right – otherwise outsource it to a pro. Your time is more productively spent in other important aspects of the business operations. If indeed you do posses the three attributes necessary to develop your own work, keep this in mind. It is human nature to believe that everything we create is a masterpiece. So before you publish your work, get some reaction from more than one objective third party and appreciate their input and proofread it several times.

One Message for Each Market

Another mistake that is often made by small business owners in the area of advertising is trying to include everything they sell in one message. This is generally done to cut expenses but it is a guaranteed way to create junk mail or ads that are totally ignored. Each target audience has unique core needs based upon demographic or psychographic characteristics; therefore, each market requires a unique message to address these needs. Readers are not willing to wade through paragraphs of material pertaining to another group's interests before reaching the copy you are directing toward them. Each target group requires a unique message and the headline must meet the test: *Is there any question as to the identity of the target audience?*

Your Company Name as a Headline?

Why do so many small business owners try to gain attention by using their name as a headline? This is the most critical part of the message. Make a point of looking at some ads in the yellow pages and flyers that come to your door and you will see that a vast majority of enterprises use their name as a headline. This is fine if your name is Nike, Sony, Ford, or Coca Cola. These companies have spent millions of dollars making these trade names a household word. So what makes most small business owners think that they can brand their own name on a shoe string budget? In actual fact, unless your name is very descriptive of the benefit that your customer can expect, this act of vanity is almost certain to create junk mail. A flyer has about four seconds to catch the attention of the target audience before it lands in the recycling bin. An effective headline or eye catching graphic is the most important part of the message. Some of the best ads I have seen don't even show the company name, just the benefits and how to obtain them.

Ad Layout Dos and Don'ts

- **Do** – create the ad or flyer message with a purpose. Think of the end result that you would like to achieve and the market being targeted then write the ad around this goal.

- **Do** – use power words of impact, value, or emotion in the headline to catch the attention of your target audience and write the body of the message to initiate action. *(See Fig. 2.5)*

- **Do** – ask a thought provoking question asking the reader to formulate an answer or make a decision favorable to your purpose.

- **Do** – utilize quality eye catching graphics to get attention whenever possible.

- **Do** – use white space generously allowing words to stand out and making reading easy.

- **Do** – let the target audience know that they are distinctly being addressed by using benefit words and making it clear – "*What's in it for them.*"

- **Do** – describe the features that differentiate your company from the competition once you have their attention answering the question, "*Why should they buy from you?*"

- **Do** – make your headline and call for action bold and large. The call for action could be dialing a phone number, checking a web site, or visiting a showroom. Once you have their attention, let your audience know clearly what it is that you want them to do.

- **Don't** – use your company name as a headline unless it is a household word. Your name or logo is not as important as the headline or call for action and should not cloud these important details.

- **Don't** – use small type and force your audience to read too much detail in an ad or flyer. Keep it brief and entice them to learn more by following your call for action.

- **Don't** – spend valuable marketing dollars on ads without first testing their effectiveness on a sample market. This could be presenting the piece to a small group of customers or objective individuals. It is much better to re-write than waste money on poor return.

Figure 2-5　　**POWER WORDS**

The following words can be used effectively with power words in headlines to get attention: you, your, how, new, who, money, now, people, want, and why. *

The following words are commonly used to effectively convey impact, value and emotion:

interest, announcing, latest, information, revolutionary, revealing, advanced, secrets, presenting, exciting, quality, appearance, exclusive, elegant, rugged, charming, durable, spectacular, lavish, imported, rare, exquisite, authentic, distinctive, proven, approval, wealth, fortune, guaranteed, profitable, tested.

* John Caples U.S. study.

2.8.2 Choosing the Right Media

Now that you have developed a great message complete with an outstanding image, where do you put it to reach your target audience? Unfortunately, there is no definitive answer regarding ad placement; however, there are methods that can be utilized to narrow the list of media vehicles for consideration. Initially, much of the media planning is educated guesswork. Trial and error analysis can be applied when there is a track record to determine the best vehicles to stay with. One of the best and simplest methods is to once again put yourself in the customer's shoes. Look at your business from the outside in, and ask the question, *"If I wanted this product or service, how would I find it?"* Ask other people. For many small businesses that sell to consumers, a Yellow Pages ad is imperative. Others may benefit as well from newspaper or radio advertising, trade publications or flyers. Most advertising vehicles such as television, radio, newspapers or magazines will provide you with a media kit. The kit should include rates, specifications and deadlines, plus demographic information on their viewers, listeners or readers. This will make it much easier to match your target market demographic with the appropriate radio station or magazine. Using many of the media described is only effective if the campaigns include enough repetition to successfully gain the desired audience response. Now, let's take a look at where some of that marketing budget can be spent. *Advertising Agencies* are used by many large companies. Most have complete in-house services including a creative department, copy writers, media buyers and production.

Signage

If you intend to attract customers to a store front, a highly visible sign is a must. The cost may be substantial and should you find the purchase cost too steep, most large signs can be rented or purchased over time. Of course, all business trucks or vans will have a sign and remember to make the web site address and tag line clearly visible. Portable signs can be used effectively on occasion to advertise specials and contractors can attract more business by conspicuously displaying "A" frame signs to announce their services at job sites.

Marketing Collateral

This is a catch phrase for material that will be available in inventory to give to prospective customers. They may be available at your office or showroom, a trade show or part of a sales person's arsenal.

- *Brochures* – can be one page or more and should be produced on a high quality stock in full color. Remember image and layout stressing benefits, features then contact and company information. Your phone and web site address should be prominent and keep in mind that if you use your name as a headline it may only be meaningful to existing customers. Color printing has become very affordable and additional runs of one or five thousand are cost effective. A note of caution – when you send out a design for print graphic layout, many studios will try to use your logo and name as a headline. It is up to you to always think like a marketer and make appropriate changes on your proof for an effective final product. Yellow pages ads are notorious for this. On-line brochures in *Adobe* .pdf format maintain excellent quality and are becoming more popular as they can be downloaded instantly from your web site.

- *Folders* – can be an excellent way of storing single leaf product panels. The advantage here is your ability to print only single pages when product information changes or becomes redundant.

- *Catalogues* – can be very expensive but necessary for many wholesale or retail businesses. If your products do not change often, consider a separate price sheet. It is easier and less expensive to print a single sheet than an entire catalogue. Check with your suppliers to see if they will share some of the production costs through co-operative advertising.

- *Rack and Post Cards* – are a popular form of collateral. Lower printing costs have made one or two sided color printing on excellent stock very affordable. People are more likely to pin these rather than an 8 ½ x 11 on a board for future reference. In fact, it is not unusual to hear from someone a year after receiving one of these cards. Again, design and final art costs may be higher than the printing.

- *Promotional Items* – such as hats, t-shirts and pens are popular give away promotional items. These are intended for branding and display your name and logo prominently. Try to find items that your customer will use in relation to your business. If you deal in computer hardware, software or operate an Internet based business then mouse pads with your name and web site address would be most appropriate. Pens are always a popular choice, but consider this; you have a very small space to print your message. Try using your web site address instead of the company name if you have a single choice. Sending someone to your site provides them with all the information they need for contact and purchasing.

Flyers

These are relatively inexpensive to produce for many businesses using their own office software. Keep in mind proper layout techniques and the purpose. Flyers are generally used for a time sensitive event, such as a sale or product clearance. They can also be printed non-commercially on your company color printer and reproduced at copy centers. There are many ways to distribute flyers and some methods are more targeted with better responses than others. Here are some suggestions for flyer distribution:

- *Newspaper Inserts* – can provide wide area coverage and is best utilized with community type papers. This method tends to be non-targeted and is ideal if your product or service satisfies a broad market. The cost can be substantial, often comparable to that of purchasing advertising space in the paper, but is more likely to be noticed.

- *Postal Walk* – allows you to cover a broad area or target specific zip and postal codes. This can be extremely useful to narrow the market and improve effectiveness. By designating certain zones for delivery, you can target businesses only if that is your market, or more affluent subdivisions should that represent your target audience. Sending a targeted message to a broad audience results in many recycled items that are costly in terms of production, delivery and a negligible return on advertising dollar. The cost per item using this method of delivery is much less than that of regular postage.

- *Hand Delivery* – is a highly targeted method of delivering your message. You can contract a company to deliver flyers to a specific area, hire a student or even family member. If you have time on weekends or evenings, this method can provide a great means of getting fresh air and exercise. You can also see for yourself if the recipient is your target customer and there may be an opportunity to make personal contact with business or homeowners. This is the lowest cost method of distributing flyers and, depending upon the business you are operating, it can be the most effective.

- *Direct Mail* – can be highly targeted and is discussed later in this chapter.

Print Ads

Advertising in print media can be very costly considering variables, such as circulation, position in the publication, number of ad insertions and the use of color. Black and white ads will be more economical than full color ads, yet somewhat less dynamic. Full page color ads on the outside back, inside front and inside back covers have the highest price tag as they are the most favorable position in magazines. A single ad insertion will be much more expensive than contracting for six or twelve editions.

- *Newspapers* – often require larger ads, such as full or half pages to grab the reader's attention. The cost can be prohibitive for a small enterprise and it is generally car dealerships, grocery stores or large chain retailers that take full pages in co-operation with their head office or supplier co-operative advertising subsidies. Smaller ads require more repetition and can often get lost in all the type. You may want to consider a regular classified ad or a business card ad in a local paper. A great headline is a must here.

- *Magazines* – are effective when matching their reader demographics to your target audience. Advertising in national magazines, because of their large circulation, can be cost prohibitive to a newly established small business. Instead, you may want to look for local publications to reach your geographic market and trade or specialty publications where the reader demographics match those of your own target market.

Television

Television is a broad reach advertising vehicle that carries the highest price tag. A small business is more likely to utilize specialty or local television broadcasting with thirty second spots going for hundreds to thousands of dollars depending on the time slot and day of the week rather than national television advertising that can cost tens of thousands of dollars and higher for thirty seconds. Production costs for some thirty second commercials developed for national television can be in excess of one hundred thousand dollars, whereas, local stations offer small businesses alternatives, including self-promotion. Ad agencies are often contracted to look after the design and production of high quality commercials for large companies. Television stations should have comprehensive media kits showing viewer numbers and demographics for different times. Other areas of television advertising that can be very costly to set up, but highly effective for the right product, are listed below.

- *Direct Response* – is a thirty or sixty second commercial that urges viewers to call a toll free number to make a purchase by credit card. Most direct response television companies require strict adherence to appropriate inventory levels.

- *Infomercials* – have a high cost for a thirty minute production and air in non-prime time spots. There are minimum standards for minimum inventory levels and order fulfillment.

- *Shopping Channels* – have high standards for inventory levels and order fulfillment. You must supply your own on air personnel or add the cost for supplied actors to your budget and adhere to rigid conditions.

Radio

Retail and service businesses can often get very good results from local radio stations. It is much easier to match radio station listener demographics to those of your target audience than it is for other media. For example, rock stations tend to have a younger listener than those playing pop or easy listening music. Radio campaigns are generally one or two weeks in duration requiring repetitions of thirty second commercials at the right time of day and the cost is much lower than television. Radio stations can produce your commercial using their own celebrities. You can also pick your own narrator or use an ad agency for a higher quality production. The significant difference using radio compared with other media is the lack of visual high impact graphics. The use of appropriate, well spoken power words is imperative to get the attention of your target audience enticing them to act upon your message. Radio marketing campaigns can also be conducted effectively in conjunction with a public relations event as local stations tend to be very community oriented and may even conduct a broadcast from the event site to attract attendees. There may be an opportunity for co-operative advertising if there is another non-competitive company involved that is willing to share the costs.

Trade Shows

There are two ways to take advantage of trade shows for promoting your business. The first is as an exhibitor and the second is as an attendee. Trade shows can play an important marketing role for *B2C* (Business to Consumer) and *B2B* (Business to Business) enterprises alike. Many industries have associations that provide valuable services to their membership including key marketing information and tools, discounted insurance rates and the annual trade show. Some of the larger shows are in the Toy and Giftware industries which can be national or global in scope. Membership in your own industry association is well worth researching. The following are some suggestions to improve trade show results for your business.

- <u>As an Exhibitor:</u>
  - o Remember image – your booth, display graphics and the appearance of your staff say a great deal about you and your business.
  - o An empty booth = lost opportunities and customers.
  - o Collect as many <u>qualified</u> names as possible and get them in to your database promptly. (*Try the fish bowl contest where visitors to your booth drop a business card in the bowl or complete a ballot to win a prize at the end of the show.*)
  - o Shows can be a good time to gather competitive intelligence.
  - o Follow up promptly with new contacts right after the show, preferably by Email, then phone or regular mail.
  - o Plan your show for achievable results. It may be more realistic to attract show visitors later to your store front for purchasing rather than having them buy at the show where inventory levels and display space are limited.
- As an Attendee:
  - o Trade shows can be an excellent networking opportunity for *B2B* operations, so match your choice of shows to your target market.
  - o Collect as many names as possible with prompt follow up afterward.
  - o Don't try to sell your product or services at the show. Exhibitors are busy growing their business so leave the actual selling until later.
  - o Attending related industry shows can also be a good way of collecting competitive information.

Web Sites

The importance of a properly developed company web site cannot be emphasized enough in a rapidly changing marketing environment that is becoming dominated more and more by new technology. This technology is driving business in the 21st Century and the web site plays a key role in achieving sales, customer satisfaction and competitive advantage. A well planned and developed site can also reduce many of the traditional costs associated with delivering your message. Some of the many objectives to consider when developing a web site for your business are:

- *Selling Products On-line* – requires a secure way to take credit card payments or existing customer credit purchases then efficiently fulfill these orders and follow up with excellent customer service.

- *Customer Service* – by providing a way for people to communicate easily with the company. This can be accomplished by publishing appropriate phones numbers and Email addresses; posting informative Q&A (Question and Answer) pages; or listing download pages for User Manuals in .pdf format. Providing these services on-line also saves the company in staff time responding to common questions.

- *Email Marketing* – to your customer database with a link to a special offer page on the web site to drive sales.

- *Sales Tools* – such as company brochures in *Adobe* .pdf format.

Unless you are operating an actual dedicated on-line business, most visitors will go to your web site because they were sent there by advertising, signs, Emails or word of mouth. The following are some of the attributes that are required for a good site:

- *Appearance* – must be outstanding and professional as this is your image. You will be judged on image; therefore, most companies outsource this important project to a professional designer and developer.

- *Content* – must be rich and current. Think of the objectives you designed into the site in the planning stage and try to put yourself in your customer's shoes to provide the appropriate content. Refresh the content on a regular basis.

- *User Friendly* – which means an effective navigation system that allows the site visitors to find the information they are looking for quickly.

- *Meet Current Standards* – as set by the W3C (*World Wide Web Consortium*). Sites must also meet professional standards which means they must be search engine friendly. Indexing bots will always like meta tags, html and text links. Do not create sites completely in Flash if you want pages to be fully indexed for high search returns.

- *Administrative Responsibilities* – are seldom understood by entrepreneurs. It is important to understand domain registration rules and trademarks, as well as the importance of contracts and doing your homework when choosing a web developer. This is for both compliance and the protection of your own intellectual property.

This topic is covered in more detail in *Section 4.2 – Creating Effective Web Sites*.

Direct Marketing

There are several ways to market your products or services directly. The development of an excellent database is the back bone for this method of promotion. In marketing, *information is power*, and the ability to collect and mine crucial customer information is a vital key in continued business growth and success.

- *Direct Selling* – involves marketing your products directly to the end user in a variety of ways including door to door; through agents hosting parties; at flea markets, events and shows; or through an elaborate method of recruiting, sometimes referred to as multi-level marketing. Use caution with the latter, often considered pyramid schemes, as many jurisdictions prohibit the use of this method of selling and recruiting.

- *Direct Mail and Catalogue* – are methods that can be very good in generating sales. Similar to other marketing techniques, these are totally database driven and since the return rate tends to be low, success is dependent upon high output numbers and a well targeted mailing list. Although this method can be used to attract new customers, it has proven to be an excellent way to up-sell existing or past customers who are familiar with your company and offering.

- *Telemarketing* – can be a rewarding method of marketing directly to the end customer or prospective customer if conducted properly. Telemarketers have a bad reputation, as we all know, for a number of reasons. Whether you engage in making the calls yourself, or hire a company to place calls on your behalf, there are some protocols and methods that should be followed to improve results. *B2C* and *B2B* enterprises can both benefit from telemarketing. The following are ways to improve your success rate using telemarketing:

o   Use a targeted database of qualified prospects whenever possible. The rate of success will be much higher and less time will be wasted on people or businesses that do not match your primary or secondary target market profiles.

o   Develop a dynamite script then memorize and practice the delivery until the words are automatic. The key here is that it should not sound like a recording. There is nothing worse than listening to an inexperienced telemarketer who fumbles through a script then needs to start from the very beginning if interrupted.

o   Always be polite and smile when you are talking.

o   Remove the prospect from your database when requested and always be cordial when ending a call regardless of the outcome.

o   Choose hours to call that will not be highly disruptive.

•   *Fax Distribution* – is usually an unwelcome activity and not recommended.

•   *Email Marketing* – has become one of the most powerful marketing tools in use but, unfortunately, one of the most abused. Spamming has become a global plague which makes it difficult for legitimate marketers to use this medium without encountering impenetrable fire walls. Email marketing is totally database driven and often integrates with your web site to produce optimal results. Listed are some of the ways to conduct successful Email marketing campaigns.

o   *Existing Customers* – are generally a safe bet to receive your Email newsletter or promotion without complaint. Try including a link in the body of the Email sending them to a contest form or an exclusive customer page on your company web site. Preferred customer offers are usually appreciated and produce good results.

o   *Opt-in* – is a requirement for ethical Email marketing. Unsolicited messages are spam – something you do not want your name attached to. *Opt-in* means that the recipient has agreed to let you send them your newsletters or special offers. This is generally done on a form submitted on-line, at time of purchase, or by submitting a contest ballot at your premises and checking the appropriate box. The double opt-in method makes your list even more robust. This authorization involves sending an Email back to confirm their permission to be on your list. The recipient must click the link in the message to confirm their *opt-in* status.

o *Inform Why* – the recipient is receiving the Email promotion. This information should be included in the first part of the message body reminding the recipient that they opted-in.

o *Personalize* – the message by putting the recipient's name and company if applicable, on the first line. Your contact management software should have the capability of performing this merge function. Keeping in mind that different markets have different needs so make the offer specific to their personal interest. Proofread the message template several times before sending – typos are a very nasty blemish on image.

o *Creative Subject Lines* – are a must to catch the reader's interest and to help penetrate spam filters. These should be brief and written like the headlines you have already created for ads. Use upper and lower case. Upper case in Email messages equates to shouting – an unacceptable practice. It is also important that the *From* line contains your company name. Also remember that spell check does not always catch subject lines so proofread carefully.

o *Avoid Excessive Use of Graphics* – as they increase the size of the message. The advent of html versus text only Email has empowered senders to change fonts, colors and insert photos in messages. Use this power judiciously as the message can get cluttered and lose its purpose.

o *Avoid Attachments* – as most people will delete the Email when viewing the header rather than opening a message with an unsolicited file that is attached. Instead, provide a link to your company web site where the file can be downloaded at their discretion.

o *Opting-out* – is the method you provide for a recipient to be removed from your list. Located at the bottom of your message, the easiest way to perform this important function is to ask them to reply to the message and type "*Remove*" in the subject line. Be sure to flag this person's name in your database (*don't delete them*) so they never receive a message again.

2.9 The Database – Managing the Marketing Effort

In examining the practices of many successful businesses, one of the common denominators is their ability to collect, store, mine and utilize key marketing data effectively. This is an area where I spend a great deal of time with clients because it has the most obvious results along with a high return on investment. The expression *Knowledge is Power* is a phrase that plays a central role in *Marketing Planning*. Sound marketing strategy and subsequent action planning is based on the collection of information that is current and rich in content. This allows companies to initiate change in a somewhat turbulent marketplace and stay focused on satisfying customer needs and changes in competitive offerings. The tool that is used to handle this valuable information is the contact database. *CRM* or *Customer Relationship Management* is a commonly used term for this type of program. *Sales Force Automation* and *Contact Management* are other terms used to describe software that performs a similar function. Technology for small business has improved dramatically and complete packaged solutions have become very affordable. There are several important features to look for when purchasing contact management software.

It is very important that the software allows you to customize fields that will be populated with information unique to your business. The power of the database is generated by filters and groups based on specific field data. For instance, if you wanted to send a personalized merge letter or Email with a special offer to all of your company's contacts using the criteria, Contact Type = *Prospects,* Industry = *Manufacturer,* State = *PA,* then you can create a filter. The filter, when activated, selects only those contacts from the database who meet these conditions allowing you to create actions targeted for them alone. You may want to send a personalized Email to all *Customers* matching a certain criteria along with a link to a page that was created on your web site where there is a special offer waiting for them alone. Of course, the program's effectiveness depends on how well you and your staff collect and input the information. The software you choose should also provide for the scheduling of calls and appointments. A user's ability to input notes when completing any form of communication with a contact is another very important feature. This improves customer service as all users have access to any communication previously made. Other features that are beneficial include integration with *Microsoft Office* products such as *Word* and *Excel* allowing the merge of database fields into documents. Most of these programs include an *import* function which eliminates tedious data entry if you can *export*, at least, basic customer information from accounting software.

Submit an Internet search using these keywords: *CRM, Customer Relationship Management, Contact Management, or Sales Force Automation,* and there will be dozens of software web sites to check out along with application comparison sites that are very useful. Study the functionality and price then match the software to your needs and resources. The following page lists three different types of contact managers available.

- *Combination Software* – such as contact managers that come pre-packaged with accounting and other industry specific software. Many of these applications lack the power and versatility of dedicated contact management applications. They offer basic functionality with the advantage of accounting integration.

- *Dedicated On-Line Solutions* – such as *salesforce.com* offer sales automation that is totally Internet driven. There are advantages to this type of solution where you pay a monthly or yearly fee for each user. The main advantage is enjoyed by organizations where their sales force is spread out in different offices or different countries. Each sales person can access the database from anywhere in the world provided they can log on to the Internet and there are no database maintenance issues with this set up. The disadvantages are possible down time if the host servers malfunction, and that you don't have physical control over your database or ownership of the software as it is hosted on a third party server.

- *Dedicated Off-Line Solutions* – are specialized applications that you purchase and install on your own computer. Some of the popular applications for small business are *Maximizer*, *ACT* by Sage and *GoldMine* *Sales & Marketing* from Front Range Solutions. I have been using *GoldMine* in my office for many years. *(See Fig. 2-6 GoldMine Screen Shot).* It is the only program that is always open on my task bar. Whenever I communicate with a contact, their record is open on the screen and I can add notes while speaking with them or refer to any previous correspondence in the history section. The software has all of the power and web integration essential to satisfy any small business requirement including: scheduling; filtering and grouping contacts for targeted mail and Email marketing; custom fields and screens; web capture from the company web site; and data exchange with *MS Word*. There are many more features that help automate office tasks. Although it has full integration capabilities with *MS Outlook*, *Goldmine* can operate with its own stand-alone Email engine which I consider a plus. *Maximizer* and *Act* are less expensive and rely on *Outlook* integration for the handling of Email. For those of you who are diehard *Outlook* users, Microsoft does offer a contact manager edition and *Prophet* by Avidian is a contact manager that fully integrates with *Outlook*, both offered at reasonable prices. Trial versions are available for most software packages by visiting the publisher's web site.

Whatever contact management route you decide to take, keep in mind the importance of communication and the collection of valuable information. Your business should be utilizing at least the same level of technology as your competitors. Initiating change amongst employees can be a challenge, particularly when new software is introduced, but once they see how easy their job becomes and the way tasks are automated, they will wonder how they ever lived without it. Some tips:

- Back up often, preferably with at least four separate media – one for each week of the month and store an extra copy off-site. It may become part of a daily backup with separate media for larger companies. This way, if a file becomes corrupt, you won't need to go too far back in time to find a clean replacement file. This method results in a minimal loss of data.

- Assign users the appropriate level of security for their position and make sure they log on and off properly as database applications don't respond favorably to improper or sudden shut down.

- Maintain your database regularly (at least monthly). Perform a pack and re-index if available, an easy task once you run the wizard and set your preferences.

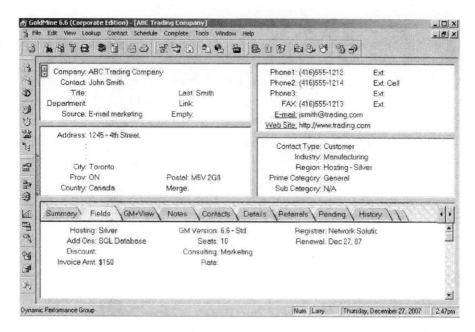

Figure 2-6   THE CONTACT MANAGER

This is the only program that is open at all times on my desktop. The contact manager is the heart of all business functions including calling and scheduling, E-mail, integration with MSOffice applications, marketing functions, reporting and automated processes. Search functions make it easy to lookup information. Note the customized fields that are specialized for this business. The contact manager you select should have similar features.

Technology and Employees

It is imperative that employees are made aware of the dangers and consequences resulting from misuse of the Internet. This includes both surfing the web and the utilization of company Email. There should be a rigid employee policy in place, in fact a condition of employment, that strict rules be followed. Serious consequences to the organization can result by visiting improper web sites and opening Email from unknown sources. I once helped a client implement strict policies after their entire computer network was shut down for days because an employee opened an attachment believing it to be from a friend. The cost in productivity and order fulfillment was staggering. Emphasize in your policy that company Email does not belong to the employee and is not for personal use. The Internet is to be used for business purposes only. Your network administrator should be able to access employee web surfing history and spot check Email usage if you find it necessary to enforce the rules which should carry a zero tolerance for abuse. Due to the fact that most networks now have constant Internet connectivity, an encrypted firewall should be in place to prevent outsiders from hacking in and virus definitions should be updated regularly. (*Preferably automatically by setting the toggle in your anti-virus software along with automatic security updates for your operating system.*)

2.10 The Marketing Budget and Media Plan

Budgeting and *Media Planning* are an integral part of the marketing plan. This section will focus on the expense side of goal setting for your plan: the total amount you will allocate to marketing, where you will spend it, and the measuring of results.

2.10.1 The Marketing Budget

It is more difficult to develop a marketing budget for a new business versus an established business with a proven track record. A new business must allocate funds to start up costs for basic first time marketing requirements such as a web site and marketing collateral including brochures and promotional items. Annual budgeting for a new *B2B*, even in the first year, is not too difficult as it will be primarily for sales tools. For a new *B2C* enterprise, it is not as straight forward. There are several ways to establish a budget:

- *Affordable Method:* Many new businesses do not have enough capital to meet all required start-up and initial operating costs. For organizations that sell to consumers, the first budget to get cut when funds are short is generally that portion of marketing that is allocated to the media plan. The result is reduced advertising exposure.

- *Built-In Cost:* Some manufacturers, distributors, or retailers will include the advertising cost as a percentage of the individual item. Similar to paying straight sales commission, this amount becomes factored in as a cost of goods.

- *Co-op Advertising:* Charged to distributors as a percentage of products sold to large retailers to produce catalogues. Also known as in-store arrangements.

- *Task Method:* Considered a separate plan where funds are allocated as a percentage of an individual campaign or project or a one-time lump sum.

- *Percentage of Sales:* The most common method of determining marketing and media budgets for established businesses is to allocate a percentage of annual sales. Retailers often utilize this method with budgets between four and seven percent of sales being common.

- *Associations:* Membership in many trade or industry associations provide member companies with industry statistics and standards along with co-operative advertising opportunities.

- *Government:* Many businesses, such as those in tourism and agriculture or fisheries, can take advantage of government subsidies for advertising.

2.10.2 The Media Plan

This is an example of a *plan within a plan.* A poorly developed *Media Plan* is another common mistake in the implementation of marketing strategy. At this stage, the *B2C* organization should have a good understanding about matching the advertising vehicle with the target audience. The tool that is utilized to schedule your ads and allocate the budget is the *Media Plan* which is created using spreadsheet software. (*See Figure 2-7.*) There will be a plan for each month with a quarterly and an annual summary. Determine every advertising vehicle that will be used and list them. Determine the rate that you must pay for each insertion of an ad, airplay for radio, the cost of promotional items or trade shows. If the total on the spreadsheet exceeds the budgeted amount, start trimming. (*A Media Plan worksheet, complete with formulas, is available with this book.*)

Failing to Measure Media Results

Failing to measure results is similar to tossing dice when it comes to establishing new budgets and *Media Plans* each year. Identifying the lead source of each new customer is the key to effective spending and maximizing your return on advertising dollar. Make a point of asking the question, *"How did you hear about us?"* Educate your employees to ask the same question and keep a scorecard. You can even attach codes to certain promotions such as coupons that identify the source. Contest ballots submitted in-store or on-line through your web site can include lead source questions making it easier to measure results. This information is critical in determining your return on advertising dollar. Cut back on media that are not producing sales and spend more on those that do.

Fig. 2-7 **MEDIA PLAN**

Media Description	January	February	March	Q1 TOTAL
Radio	$ 300.00	$ 300.00	$ 400.00	$1,000.00
Magazine 1	$ 400.00	$ 300.00	$ 400.00	$1,100.00
Magazine 2	$ 325.00	$ 325.00	$ 325.00	$ 975.00
Newspaper2	$ 150.00	$ 150.00	$ 150.00	$ 450.00
Web Maintenance	$ 50.00	$ 50.00	$ 50.00	$ 150.00
Yellow Pages	$ 125.00	$ 125.00	$ 125.00	$ 375.00
Flyers - Direct Mailing	$ 100.00	$ 100.00	$ 100.00	$ 300.00
Trade Show			$ 900.00	$ 900.00
Association Dues		$ 250.00		$ 250.00
TOTALS	**$1,450.00**	**$1,600.00**	**$2,450.00**	**$5,500.00**

The Media Plan, Figure 2-7, details all advertising vehicles for a selected period of time showing the cost for each. It is important to track monthly, quarterly and annual projected spending. This is a simplified example of a quarterly spreadsheet. It lacks the detail and the balance of annual projections found on the formatted MS Excel template available with this book. Similar to the Profit & Loss projections, it is important to compare actual monthly, quarterly, and annual results against your projected budget. It is also possible to track lead source percentages on the spreadsheet to analyze which vehicles are generating the most business. Another great benefit from spreadsheets is the ability to create various line or bar trending charts from results. This makes it easy, at a glance, to track quarterly or annual spending along with comparisons to sales.

2.11 Personal Selling

There are very few consumer products or services that require a salesperson to assist in completing the exchange. Automobiles, real estate, life insurance and some financial services such as investments are part of a very short list consumers are unlikely to purchase without external motivation or help with regulatory compliance. If you have a business that sells to consumers, the primary method of promotion is likely to be advertising, so be prepared with the extra start-up capital to satisfy the *Media Plan*.

If you operate a company that sells products or services to other businesses, your primary method of promotion will be personal selling, and no other method comes close to producing the same results. Think about it – with few exceptions, everything a company buys to fuel its industrial fire has a sales person managing the account. Stationery and office supplies, raw materials, telecommunication services, and the list goes on. This is a hard realization for new entrepreneurs starting up a *B2B* enterprise as not everyone is capable of making a cold call. The greatest business idea in the world will have a slim chance of success if the owner or one of the partners can't sell. "*Then, I will spend more money on advertising,*" many new *B2B* entrepreneurs will say. Unfortunately, the amount needed to brand a new company successfully is prohibitive for most people. The phone will not ring! Others will say, "*Since I am not comfortable making the calls myself, I will just hire a sales person.*" Ask how much they are prepared to pay and most would say that they would remunerate their new account executive with a commission. Here is where reality should start to sink in. Where are you going to find such a person? The truth is, all of the really good sales people are already working and making a ton of dough. Unless you are prepared to pay a substantial guaranteed base salary, the chances of finding an experienced sales person willing to take a chance on a new and unproven idea are slim at best. This only leaves one person and you are the one who needs to make it happen!

Although strong selling skills are a must for *B2B* entrepreneurs, they are also an important asset for anyone in business from management to front line employees. Selling skills play an important role, not only in all forms of business, but in our personal lives as well. Anyone who has gone for a job interview or negotiated a large purchase can attest to that. There are different types of sales people. The showroom salesperson, most often related to retail, must have excellent closing skills. Telemarketers should have good cold calling techniques and in some cases excellent closing skills. Outside sales people who are selling products and services to other businesses generally require the entire package. In addition to being cold calling and closing experts, they must also be great at prospecting and making presentations. This section will cover all aspects of sales. Most of the methods and theories presented here are not new. Good selling skills are built on a foundation of basic but effective principles that do work.

2.11.1 Developing Selling Skills

There are a number of attributes that contribute to the development of good selling skills, some of which can be learned from books, classrooms or successful sales people willing to share their experience and knowledge in a role as coach and mentor. There are certain personalities that are more likely to make good sales people. It does not mean that shy, introverted individuals will fail as a rep, it is just that they may have to work a little harder and talk to more prospects. These people may also become much better at selling than their extraverted counterparts if some of the other necessary character traits listed below are adopted.

The _80 : 20 Rule_ will be referred to a number of times in this section. This rule rings true in many disciplines, especially sales, where twenty percent of your over-achieving people write eighty percent of the business.

- _Psychology_ - understanding human behavior and resigning yourself to the fact that people do not want to be sold anything. Successful sales people are masters at the art of using psychology to their advantage making the sale a logical conclusion in a series of pre-defined steps.

- _Listening_ – is by far the most important character trait of a good sales person. While working in sales management for a large multi-national corporation, I was responsible for hiring, training and coaching a large department comprised of telesales personnel who sold and serviced smaller accounts; account managers who only serviced large customers; and outside sales people who utilized great prospecting, cold calling, presentation and closing skills to bring large customers on board. In the recruiting process, when the list was trimmed at the interview stage, one of the questions that the candidates were asked was to name the three main character traits a good sales person should possess. Common answers included people skills, communication skills and others that are important, but if <u>listening</u> was not part of the answer they gave, then the recruiting process often ended there.

- *<u>Telling is not Selling</u>* – is one of the primary reasons a majority of sales people are in the eighty bracket of the *80 : 20* rule. Eighty percent are under achievers for a number of reasons, one of which is that instead of listening to a prospect to learn more about their problems and needs, they are reading from a company brochure and explaining about all of the products or services offered whether applicable or not. So long as the rep is talking or telling, they are not selling. Actual selling only takes place when a rep is <u>listening</u> to customer needs after asking the right questions.

- *<u>Product / Service Knowledge</u>* – can make the difference between a good and a poor sales person. Benefits and features, the important concepts developed in the early marketing planning stages, must be fully understood to apply against customer needs and competitive offerings in order to close a sale. A person who has mastered the fundamental selling skills need only learn the product and enthusiastically believe in the solutions provided to sell anything effectively.

- *<u>Scripts</u>* – are the most effective tool for learning to cold call and make presentations. Scripts must be well written and practiced until they are second nature. There is nothing worse than listening to a sales person who is reading from a script. More on this important topic later.

- *<u>Self-Confidence</u>* – without it selling is almost impossible unless you talk to enough people and engage one who feels sorry for you. Would you buy from a sales person who did not exhibit self-confidence? Highly unlikely! Self-confidence is a state of mind created by knowledge. You must believe in yourself and the product or service and trust that you are doing people a favor by introducing them to your solution, whether they buy or not. At least they will know about it. Self-confidence cannot be learned or taught. Even people who are very shy can be self-confident. Developing better presentation skills by joining a *Toastmasters* type of club and reading self development material are ways to improve. I enjoy a number of speakers; however, my favorite on personal development is Jim Rohn. I remember attending a weekend seminar he conducted in Toronto and taking two books of notes. After studying his books, tapes and videos, I changed many of the things that I was doing and the ways that I did them. Find your own favorite, and remember, be self-confident but not arrogant.

Stages of Sales Skills Development

An interesting model that I was introduced to many years ago by some of my early career sales trainers brings the learning process together very well. It divides the skills development process into four distinct stages of competence. A quicker progression through the stages results in a better closing ratio meaning more sales and fewer calls required to meet objectives.

Stage 1: Unconscious Incompetence is a state where a new sales person with no previous training is released on an unsuspecting list of prospective customers. Although they are eager, most of the time they are just telling and not selling. Of course, this results in few sales.

Stage 2: Conscious Incompetence is the next phase where our budding rep has learned the basic principles of selling but they forget to apply them, still resulting in few sales. Skill development often ends at the second or third stage. Reps like this are found in the eighty percent bracket and look for work often.

Stage 3: Conscious Competence is a state where a maturing sales person understands the principles behind effective selling and they are applied with much deliberation. Sales begin to build rapidly.

Stage 4: Unconscious Competence is the final stage whereby your rep is selling to needs and answering objections properly without giving the response a second thought. These are your high achievers that are found in the twenty percent bracket. They are the individuals who get the bonuses, win the contests, get the recognition and make you look good. They all have work!

2.11.2 Prospecting

The first step to successful selling is to conduct effective prospecting activities. Prospecting is the act of collecting qualified names to add to your database for the purpose of converting them to customers.

- *Qualifying Prospects:* Look back at the initial marketing research conducted when developing your marketing strategy and review the profile you created of your primary customer. For most *B2B's*, this means segmenting the market geographically, by industry, and by business size. You want to spend your quality time going after the perfect customer. This may be a manufacturer within a certain distance of your office that has ten to twenty employees. It doesn't mean you won't sell to a small corner shop with one or two employees. It means you won't be adding them to your list of qualified prospects as they are likely to be a waste of time.

- *Business Buying Hierarchy:* It is imperative to identify the individuals who make the buying decisions. The first call should be to the person identified as the *Decision Maker*. Other members of this buying group are the *Influencer*, the *User*, and the *Gatekeeper*. When I sold accounts receivable management services to businesses, the credit manager was only an influencer and they were easy to get an appointment with. Unfortunately, however, they could seldom sign a contract meaning that a great deal of time was wasted trying to pitch to them alone. A repeat visit was almost always necessary to meet and close the deal with their boss. Top sales people will always start with the Decision Maker, in this case the VP of Finance, or in a smaller company, the President. They are the people who identify with the bottom line. The president may ask you to speak with the manager, and that is fine. It is now very easy to introduce yourself to the Influencer and ask if the Decision Maker can sit in. At least if a return visit is necessary, you have already identified yourself and your company to the most important contact. The Influencer must still be sold, because as their position in the pecking order dictates, the president will value this person's opinion and possibly that of a user. The Gatekeeper is often a receptionist or administrative assistant and these people can be great at opening doors for you or keeping them shut.

- *Prospect Lists:* The great thing about operating a *B2B* versus a *B2C* is that there are many sources of lists for businesses and they are much easier to acquire than consumer prospecting lists. Company name, industry, full address, phone, fax, contact names (decision maker and influencer if possible), Email, and web site are all part of the basic list of information that should populate the fields in the contact management database. Electronic lists are the best, of course, because the export and import functions eliminate hours of data input from print directories. This isn't always possible so consider paying a student if manual input is required as your time is better spent selling and managing your business.

Sources of lists include:

o   _Chambers of Commerce_ – most of which produce annual directories that often include all of the information required for the prospect database. Although it is generally advantageous to become a member of a local chamber, it is not always necessary in order to purchase their member directory.

o   _Trade Associations_ – like chambers offer great advantages to industry members including member directories which are excellent for networking as well as prospecting.

o   _Business Directories_ – that are published regularly for different geographic regions in North America are available in print and on-line. Conduct a web search using the keywords '_business directories_' and a number of quality sites will be returned. Some are free but the good ones will charge a fee and the cost may be worth the investment to enrich your database. Using keywords that include the '_city name_' and '_businesses_' often return local directories that can be useful.

o   _Dun and Bradstreet_ and _Financial Post_ – publish Fortune 100 and 500 company information.

o   _Economic Development Departments_ – of local municipalities often publish business directories and statistics.

Other Sources: There are many other ways to prospect and the top sales people will always be in prospect mode armed with their business cards and a notepad. The following are other methods of obtaining names for follow up calls.

o   _Trade Shows_ – collecting business cards by running a fish bowl draw and other contests.

o   _Club Memberships_ – such as golf and country clubs offer an excellent way to prospect for new business. Remember not to try to make the sale while prospecting – it is meant to introduce you to a prospect for a follow up call. If you are discussing business on the golf course, don't talk shop on the first, second, seventeenth or eighteenth holes.

o _Newspapers_ – especially business papers are a great source for discovering qualified new prospects for your database. Check the ads and the editorials.

o _Drive By_ – and scout commercial or industrial areas while you are on the road. This adds another dimension to your prospecting as you can see the prospect's place of business and qualifying them is easy. Instead of taking the short-cut to your next sales call (_unless you are late_) detour through the commercial park and write down some names. Look also at the names on delivery trucks. If they could be a prospect write down the name and phone number and match them against your database when you return to the office. This is also a good way of adding names or staying on top of the competition.

2.11.3 Cold Calling

Cold calling is simply the act of making contact with a person that you have never met to introduce your company along with its products and services. The purpose of this initial contact can be to make a sale over the phone; however, the call is more commonly made to set up a meeting with a prospect to make a formal sales presentation. The method of cold calling that automatically comes to mind is the frightening telephone call to a stranger. Although this is by far the most effective method of contact, there are other ways to introduce your offering.

• _Introduction Letters:_ Most new _B2B_ entrepreneurs will give this a try before picking up the telephone. Actually, most will try anything before picking up the telephone. My experience has been that letters are a major waste of time and money. They only prolong the inevitable and delay sales as well as valuable cash flow. A well written letter can have a response rate that is a fraction of one percent, so it is strictly a numbers game. Let's examine the routine your letter will follow once you put a stamp on it. The mail arrives at the prospect's office and is sorted. Hopefully your message goes to the decision maker but often it is opened or discarded as junk mail before reaching them. If the decision maker does get the letter and looks at it, you have two seconds to catch their attention before it lands in the recycling bin or shredder. Even if your letter gets some initial attention, the reader will likely file it in a tray on their desk where it will start to get buried by other documents while they deal with tasks and responsibilities that are urgent or important. When you call them in a week and ask them if they had a chance to read your letter, the answer will almost always be, "What letter?", or, "No, I didn't get it." If you insist on trying this method of introduction, these suggestions may give your letter a better chance to break the ice.

o   Personalize the label and letter to the primary decision maker. This relates directly back to the thorough prospecting exercise you conducted and the quality of data input to your contact management database.

o   Keep it brief. Get used to the fact that people (absolutely everyone as you will find out) are always too busy and won't have time to read a novel.

o   Use benefit words to get their attention and state clearly, *what's in it for them.*

o   Remember the purpose of the letter and state the call for action. Example: *I will call you next week to discuss your company's objectives and determine if our solutions may be a fit.*

o   <u>Do</u> schedule them for a follow up and make the call when promised.

On the subject of Email instead of snail mail - don't even think about it? Email that is unsolicited is spam, plain and simple, and is a totally unacceptable business practice. Sending unsolicited faxes is another method that is unacceptable.

• *Drop In:* Most prospects do not welcome uninvited sales calls. A drop in can be utilized with great success if you are delivering a flyer or other piece of marketing collateral and looking for the name of the appropriate contact person for your database. In this case, it is quite acceptable to ask the receptionist for the name of the appropriate decision maker. Do not expect to get an immediate audience with them, although it may happen on occasion. Instead, get their business card and the vital contact information for the contact manager then schedule a follow up call. Leave a flyer or brochure to their attention. There will be times when the gatekeeper follows orders not to entertain any solicitation so be mindful and respect the *No Soliciting* signs.

The Benefit Statement

This is a statement comprised of one or two sentences that clearly describes your company through the use of appropriate benefit words, "W*hat's in it for the customer?*" It is also known as an elevator or networking speech because it is brief and will generate a high level of interest from a prospect who asks what you do. For instance, a human resources consultant in a networking setting with a room filled with qualified prospects is chatting with several people in a group and one of them asks, "*And what line of work are you in?*" One answer may be, "*I am a human resources consultant.*" How exciting is that? Someone who read this book and developed a good benefit statement may reply, "*My company helps small businesses retain employees and obtain higher levels of productivity.*" Everyone in the group that has employees will most certainly want to learn more about these services that have such a positive impact on the bottom line. This statement will also become an integral part of the cold calling telephone script and benefit words should be used whenever possible in all communications with prospects.

Developing a Dynamite Script

The key to successful cold calling is to have a great script then practice delivering it until the sound is natural and never like you are reading verbatim from a screen or a piece of paper. These are also known as branching scripts because they take into consideration every response imaginable from your prospect and the appropriate way to continue the dialogue, always with the purpose of the call in mind. The purpose of the call must be clearly understood before starting your cold calling script development. The goal of your communication with each prospect is to ultimately convert them to customers, however in most cases, the purpose of the initial telephone cold call is to secure an appointment. It is also important to remember that you should start calling at the top of the decision making hierarchy to take advantage of benefit words in the script that address the bottom line. This way the speech is directed at an individual who really cares about profitability, and if approached properly, they will make time to hear about your solution.

Tangible Products vs. Conceptual Services

There is a substantial difference between selling products, tangible items that can be seen, felt, weighed and measured versus selling a service that is conceptual. My sales background has included selling products. However, the majority of my sales experience has been in conceptual selling from consumer life insurance and estate planning to accounts receivable management then consulting services. It is much more difficult to sell a concept than it is a widget. The sale of products usually starts with price comparison. Since quality is generally not the issue, service can be your key selling point. To get your foot in the door it will be important not to make the prospect believe that you are trying to bump their existing supplier right away. Instead you only make them believe that you want to show them an alternative source of supply. Once you get your foot in the door and make a presentation, the primary goal will most certainly be to replace their existing supplier with your product.

In conceptual selling, the prospect generally needs an emotional stimulation to buy as they can only visualize the benefits through a state of mind. Consultants sell a conceptual service where benefits are a state of mind and the return on investment cannot be guaranteed. By utilizing good selling techniques, a prospect can be stimulated to purchase by painting a picture and putting them in it, then bringing them out by applying your solutions to their newly discovered problems. For the balance of this section, I will use the conceptual example of the human resources consultant that was mentioned earlier with the networking speech. Many people are leaving long terms of employment to start up consulting practices in a variety of specializations.

Stages of the Initial Telephone Cold Call

The initial call is made up of a series of stages that will be reflected in the script. For this example, the primary target market would likely be a business with twenty to fifty employees. Fewer than twenty would probably be too small to justify an H.R. service and over fifty would likely have their own specialist. Substitute the fictitious information in these examples with statements and questions applicable to your business and industry.

o   *Introduction* – "Hello, my name is Jennifer MacDonald from HR Consulting Services." Straight forward introduction.

- o *Benefits* – "Our company helps businesses improve their bottom line by increasing employee productivity." Keep it brief. Note the benefit words: improve, increase. Other words may include save, make, protect, reduce. Compile your own list of benefit words that suit your business.

- o *Purpose* – "The reason for my call is to set up a brief meeting with you to discuss our services." Cut to the chase – the president of the company will appreciate your candor in getting right to the point as they are always very busy and don't have time for lengthy discussions with strangers. Stick with the purpose – to get an appointment.

- o *Branching Script* – begins at this stage as responses will vary.

Branching the Script

At this point in the call, the chances of the prospect grabbing their day timer and saying, "Sure, when do you want to meet?" is as likely as being struck by lightning. Your script must list every possible response and the way you will reply to it. The *GoldMine* software that I use has a powerful branching script function where a script can be written and the responses (*valuable marketing information*) are automatically populated into custom fields with a single click. List the possible responses to your request for a meeting.

"I'm not interested?"   Many people would fold up like jelly at this point and say, *"Sorry to bother you."* If you stop here, immediately head for the nearest news stand and start looking through the want ads. The moment you give up on a call, consider that prospect lost. The correct reply here should be, *"Can you tell me why you are not interested?"*

Do not make statements as they tend to put people on the defensive. Always ask questions. Now, there may be several responses to your reply above.

"We don't need it." or *"We have someone to perform those duties."* In formulating your replies, keep the purpose in mind – to get an appointment. Don't get in to lengthy explanations or attempt to sell your services during the call. You might try these replies:

Scenario 1:

"*We don't need it.*"   "*Do you have employees?*"

"*Yes*"   "*I'm not trying to say at this point that you do need our services. I can do a quick analysis that is free of charge and let you know almost immediately if we can help your profitability. Is your day timer handy? What day is good for you?*"

"*No*"   "*It would appear that we really can't help you in that case. Thank you for your time.*"

In the first instance of Scenario 1, you are re-qualifying the prospect. If they have employees, unless there is a full time specialist on staff, they will have a need for your service. If they reply no, it is the end of the road with this one and obviously you did not do a very good job at qualifying them initially. You may also want to ask them how many employees they have at some point. Note how all replies lead back to the purpose of the call. Let's continue the dialogue in this scenario.

"*We have great employees.*"   "*I'm sure you do. There are many areas in employee relations where we can help companies. Not only to improve productivity, but also protection from non-compliance with government regulations. There is no obligation to simply discuss these important issues. How is Monday afternoon, or would Tuesday morning be better?*"

"*How do you do this?*"   Be careful here. Most sales people will start giving a long description about their services. The more you talk – the greater the chance of losing the appointment as you are providing more reasons for the prospect to object. Try this:

                               "*There are so many ways that we can help businesses. This makes it almost impossible for me to match a solution for you over the telephone and that is why I want to set up a brief meeting. Which day is best for you?*"

Stick to the purpose!

"How much will this cost?"   This is another response that can get you into trouble. You don't want to talk dollars at this point and you certainly can't say, *"I'm not telling you."* Try something like this:

"It is difficult to put an exact dollar figure on our solutions as our services are customized to unique client needs. I can say that our customers do get a substantial return on their investment."

Note the use of the word *investment* instead of cost. Although the customer can write off the services as a business expense, get into the habit of calling it an investment and use the term *Return on Investment* (ROI).

The important thing to emphasize in dealing with this scenario is that the prospect has absolutely nothing to lose by meeting with you and possibly much to gain by looking at your services. There may not be a fit, but most likely if there are more than twenty employees without a qualified specialist on staff, many areas of employee relations may be neglected. These could include a high turnover rate due to poor motivation and working conditions along with the associated cost to recruit and train. Employers also need protection against possible financial loss due to non-compliance with multiple pieces of complex government legislation on employee relations and the work place. It is important not to end a scenario dialogue prematurely as the sale is lost at that point. Only say enough during each response to get back to the appointment setting line. Remain tenacious but not annoying; in other words, know when to pack it in and go on to the next call. Asking questions rather than making statements keeps the tone low and you won't sound overbearing as many telemarketers do. You are bound to speak with the odd person who is totally ignorant, but you will be surprised at how few there will be.

Scenario 2:

"We have someone."   *"Is this person on staff?"*

It is important to ascertain if the human resources person the prospect alludes to is a member of the staff or an outsourced person such as another consultant. Our script will branch in two possible directions here, as 2a or 2b.

Scenario 2a:

"They are on staff."   What position does this person hold?"

It is unlikely that the person the prospect is referring to is an HR specialist. If indeed they are, there would be no need to continue as your service is not currently required. You may want to provide the prospect with your company information and mark them down for a follow up call in six months or a year in case their situation changes.

"It is our office manager."   "Would you agree that it is difficult to be a specialist when you wear a number of hats? As an objective third party, we can provide you with a no charge analysis in all areas of employee relations that can affect profitability. How is Tuesday morning or is Wednesday afternoon better for you?"

Again, your reply should have limited matters of fact or statements. Revert back to questions or probes to keep the session alive. It is important not to make the office manager's position feel threatened.

Scenario 2b:

"They are outsourced."   "Are you pleased with the work they are doing for you?" then "Are there any areas you feel that are being overlooked?"

In this case you don't want to come across as if you are trying to bump the prospect's existing consultant. Your appeal to the prospect will be to show an alternative in case something happens to their existing supplier.

Cold Calling Tips

- *Practice:* Then practice and practice some more. Memorize your script and make it sound natural. If possible, try recording your performance then play it back. There is no better way than this to improve your delivery.

- *Role Play:* With someone playing the part as the prospect acting out different scenarios. Record yourself then play it back and fine tune the mistakes.

- *Smile:* When you are speaking try using a mirror. Believe it or not, the person on the other end can tell if you are smiling. When I was working as a rep selling accounts receivable services, the office was only used for making calls to set up appointments and delivering signed contracts. Each rep had a small cubicle with a telephone. I -9was the top sales person in the country at the time with a good closing ratio and never had a problem getting appointments. One day I was making cold calls at about 9am and one of our other top reps was making calls on the other side of the cubicle wall. I struck out on my first five calls then I heard a voice from the other side say, "You're not smiling!" She was absolutely right. I had a short coffee break, took a deep breath, put a smile on my face then started again and set five appointments in the next ten calls.

- *Stalling:* Prospects who stall can really waste your time. If someone says, "*I am busy, call me back,*" give them the benefit of a return call one time only. Remind them that they asked you to call back and if they continue to stall, you are probably wasting your time.

Scheduling

Picking up the telephone to make the first call is one of the toughest things you will ever do. Even the top sales reps in the twenty percent bracket will admit it is one of the hardest things they do. It is easy to get side tracked with other menial tasks and activities always thinking, I'll make some calls later, or maybe tomorrow. Ouch! No calls mean no appointments which equates to no sales thus creating the greatest motivator for new entrepreneurs – poverty or working for someone else! Actually, once you muster up the nerve and dial the first number, it does get better. In fact, after the first call or two, it can be fun especially when you get some appointments. The key here is discipline and great time management. Again, referring to the *Seven Habits*, the fundamentals of sound time management are illustrated by Covey extremely well. Concentrate on the important tasks and issues. Making sales calls will be the most important task at hand for a majority of *B2B* entrepreneurs. Avoid procrastinating and just pick up the phone and remind yourself that you have a great offering and people need to learn about it.

The best way to avoid the evil of procrastination is to block out certain portions of each day strictly for making calls. You can determine the best times to reach your decision makers. Forget about Monday mornings and Friday afternoons for obvious reasons. Your weekly schedule may show blocks of three hours set aside Tuesday morning, Wednesday afternoon and Thursday morning just to make prospecting cold calls. To get around highly motivated gatekeepers, try calling your prospect before or after regular hours. Company owners and presidents generally put in longer hours. Learn how to deal with voice mail and determine for yourself whether or not you should leave a message. Prospects seldom return a message left from a cold calling salesperson thus many good salespeople just call until they get a real voice. If you have call display enabled on your line, it might be a good idea to leave a message because you have been identified anyway.

Keeping Score

As in most business functions, if you can't measure it – you can't manage it! I found this to be absolutely true both as a sales rep and as a sales manager. As a rep, I needed to know how many calls were needed to get an appointment and how many appointments I needed to get a sale. Selling is a numbers game and knowing these figures allowed me to set up each week or month for the right amount of calling and presentation activity to meet and exceed my goals. As a sales manager, objectives in the form of numbers were set each week, month and quarter for each team and each member of the team. These numbers would start with a dollar amount, for example $15,000 per month as a minimum quota before hitting bonus levels. If the average sale was $1,500 then ten sales were required each month. If it took the average sales rep four appointments to make a sale, then forty appointments were required each month to qualified prospects, or ten per week. This is the closing ratio, and in this case it would be 1:4 (one sale in four appointments). If the average sales person needed to make four calls to get an appointment, it would again be a ratio of 1:4 (one appointment in four calls). They would be required to make one hundred and sixty telephone calls in a month or forty calls per week to meet their sales objectives. Dividing the monthly sales by the number of calls to achieve that goal equates to each telephone call being worth $9.38, and in sales terms it is definitely *dialing for dollars*.

When sales people progress through the stages of competency, as their skills improve, so will their ratios. A new rep may have a closing ratio of 1:8 after a month. In sales, the learning curve or training period could be three to six months at which time a ratio that is close to average would be expected. Some of the top reps, those in the twenty percentile discussed earlier, would have ratios well above average, possibly 1:2.5 which translates to fewer calls for more sales. These people don't need to work as hard as the average rep to achieve the same results because they have developed better selling skills. Some sales people can never reach the same plateau of skills for a number of reasons. These reps will always need to work harder, putting in more activity to achieve the required results. If they have the drive and the heart, there is no reason why these people can't make a very significant contribution to the organization.

Ratios and Sales Rep Development

If you find your business growing with the addition of sales people, it is important to be able to measure all aspects of a rep's performance. The numbers will clearly show how a new sales person is progressing through the stages of skill competence. The business owner or sales manager will match monthly and quarterly performance against assigned objectives, or quota. If the results meet or exceed the objective regularly, a good supervisor would probably give the rep a little more autonomy as these are the twenty percent. They should also be rewarded with money (bonuses) and recognition. If a rep is not achieving revenue goals then look at their activity, starting with the number of appointments in the month. If the salesperson is making the average requirement of forty visits to new prospects, the indication would be that their closing ratio was too low. The manager would then know to concentrate coaching efforts on assisting with presentation and closing skill improvement. If the monthly number of visits was less than objective, the number of calls would then be scrutinized. If the calls meet objective then coaching would concentrate on calling skills and the script, possibly utilizing role play with other members of the sales team. If the total calls are below the objective number, it is a clear indication that the rep has not put in enough of an effort. After a fiscal quarter of under achievement a warning letter could be issued indicating that the next quarter would be used to measure and decide their future. (One month or even one fiscal quarter does not necessarily show a trend. In most cases, two fiscal quarters are definite indicators of trending.) Accurate measuring requires the two key ingredients of *numbers* over *time*, in this case, $ each month or $ each quarter.

Figure 2-8   SALES CALL SHEET

Day of the Week	Calls to Decision Makers	Appointments Set	Sales
Monday	6	1	0
Tuesday	12	3	1 / $1,200
Wednesday	8	2	0
Thursday	14	3	1 / $900
Friday	8	1	2 / $2,200
TOTALS	**48**	**13**	**4 / $4,300**

The Sales Call Sheet, Figure 2-8, is one of the worksheets available with this book. It is in MS Excel 97-2003 format. There is a sheet for a single week, one for a single month, and another for a fiscal quarter all with formulas including ratio calculation. One week, or even one month are too short a time period to measure ratios effectively. The results from one, or preferably two quarters more accurately reflect accurate results and trending. Trending can easily be displayed on charts.

2.11.4 Presentation and Closing

You've done a great job so far. Sound marketing planning provided a profile of your perfect customer. This allowed you to prospect effectively adding hundreds of qualified names to your database. Then an effective script was developed based on powerful benefit words, practiced to perfection and released on an unsuspecting populace with tremendous results. Now that you have all these appointments, what's next? Back to the 80 : 20 rule. Some of the residents in the majority group on a sales team will be very good at calling and getting quality appointments, but their low numbers in signed contracts are a clear indication that there is a lack of solid presentation and closing skills. What a shame to play great for three quarters then throw it away with a poor performance near the end of the game.

Top sales people, those in the twenty percentile, have a very high closing ratio which means they don't need to work as hard to produce the numbers. This section describes the stages in a presentation that will lead to successful methods of closing and ways to handle objections effectively. These principles are not new but they are proven and most of the content works equally as well for outside sales reps and show room retail sales people alike. Many aspects of these closing skills can also be applied to telemarketing and other forms of negotiation including employee relations and dealing with difficult people.

Tips and Techniques

- *Arrive Early and Be Prepared:* Imagine all of the time and hard work to get an appointment with a first rate prospect then showing up at their office fifteen minutes late! Not a good first impression and if they will still see you, you will need to make it quick. Early doesn't mean half an hour where you are wasting your time and making the prospect feel uncomfortable. I think five minutes is cutting it close so my practice was to arrive in the parking lot fifteen minutes early and check in with reception ten minutes prior, announcing that I was a little early and didn't mind waiting. While waiting, I would take advantage of the opportunity to read and collect their marketing collateral, take note of any civic or industry awards displayed, and observe the people passing by to get a feel for their corporate culture. Prior to the meeting date, I would have done some research on the prospect's company and industry. The Internet is an ideal tool for this task as most companies have a very comprehensive web site. Prospects appreciate having someone speak their language so the homework and on-site observations can be used to great advantage in understanding their specific needs.

- *Appearance:* Professional, plain and simple. It is acceptable to dress down to the prospect's business culture, especially after they become a client. My suggestion would be, never below a business casual standard for either gender and in some industries a business suit.

- *Self-Confidence:* Would you buy from a person who is not confident? Of course not, and this important personal characteristic is well worth repeating. Knowledge, feeling good about yourself and the solution you have to present are usually all it takes. Always assume that the prospect is going to buy and you will be leaving with a sale more times than not. This will help to keep confidence high. The prospect is buying you as a trusted solution provider as much as they are buying your product or service. Although self-confidence is a necessity, be careful not to come across as being too cocky or arrogant.

- *Enthusiasm:* Have you ever noticed how many people arrive at work without smiling and whenever asked, *"How are you?"* the reply is *"Not bad!"* Isn't that a terrible personal state of mind? As a manager, I noticed this behavior quite often. Can you guess which group acted this way? You've got it, the eighty percent doing twenty percent, and no wonder. The under achievers are in the office early displaying little enthusiasm with a cup that is half empty. The over achievers are out in the field selling with a ton of enthusiasm and a cup that is always half full. Ask them how they are doing and the answer will always be, *"Great!"*, even if they aren't feeling well. No wonder they get all the perks!

- *Control the Meeting:* This is your *"dog and pony show"* and if you don't control the meeting you are wasting your time. Stay focused, stick to the game plan and ask the right questions. Small talk or discussions off topic are alright in small doses but get the meeting back on track quickly because you are unlikely to get a second chance.

- *Silence Can Be Golden:* You may be asking some tough questions and the answers could be the key to signing the contract. If you break the silence before the prospect has the opportunity to answer honestly, it could be time to pack up. Keep this tip in mind when you ask for the sale.

- *Paint a Picture:* Remember the psychology aspect discussed earlier. Most people exhibit a natural resistance to purchasing and that is especially true with conceptual offerings. It is the sales person's ability to create the right level of emotion that provides the stimulus for the prospect to make a buying decision. This is done during the probing stage discussed in detail later, where a good sales rep paints a vivid picture associated with the problem or potential problem and puts the prospect in it. The skilled sales pro will then bring the prospect out of the picture with their solution.

- *Ask for the Sale:* This may sound obvious but it is a big problem with many sales people. A great job through all the stages can be wasted if you don't ask for the sale.

- *Don't Talk Yourself Out of the Sale:* I have seen many sales reps lose a sale because they wouldn't stop talking. There will be opportunities to go back and up sell this new customer.

The Stages

There are a number of theories that have different names with similar methods and results. The theory I learned early in sales was the <u>AIDCA</u> method. It is very effective and I have been teaching it ever since. Each initial stands for a stage in the presentation process.

- **Attention** – Simply identify yourself and your company to the prospect at the start of the meeting. This period will only take up a few minutes and may include some small talk based on a photo or item in the room that indicates a shared interest. Avoid getting into lengthy discussions that are likely to sidetrack the objective – to get a sale.

- **Interest** – The second stage of the presentation is the last time you will speak without asking a question. In the *Interest* stage, briefly describe your company activities in terms of benefits for the client. This may include a short history, company expertise and accomplishments using benefit words. The total elapsed time to the end of this stage should be no more than five minutes. Now it is time to sell. From now on, you will be asking questions. At this point it is recommended that you ask the prospect if it is alright to ask some questions about their company. They will almost always comply and the stage is set for the most important phase of the presentation.

- **Desire** – Also known as the probing phase of the presentation, this is where you make it or break it. As a sales manager, I would travel with my sales people whenever they needed help in any area. These reps were almost always in the eighty percentile and from evaluating their numbers most often they were pretty good at prospecting and getting appointments but terrible at closing. I would try to be a fly on the wall while they were doing their presentation and found it very difficult at times not to interrupt and tell them blatantly to shut up! Unlike their over achieving associates in the twenty percentile bracket who were very good at asking the right questions then listening intently, these reps got the stage and wouldn't give up the microphone. Quite often these long winded orators would read verbatim from each brochure on every company product or service whether the prospect needed them or not. At the end, the victim would comment that it was a great presentation but they really mean to say, "*Don't call me, I'll call you.*" It is during this phase that a good sales person will discover problems within the organization and the prospect's willingness to do something about it. Ten minutes into this stage, and the sales person should have a pretty good idea if the prospect is likely to buy. This may be a good time to pack up and move on if you feel honestly that the prospect does not need your offering or if their character type is one you could not work with.

- **Conviction** – This stage is characterized by presenting the prospect with a summary of the issues discussed and obtaining their agreement with the findings along with a conviction to improve the situation, preferably with your solution.

- **Action** – The closing phase where the prospect takes action by signing a contract or agrees to take the sales cycle to the next level.

Needs Analysis

Needs Analysis is the most important part of selling and corresponds to the **D**esire stage of the presentation. In this case it is a meeting with a prospect in their office, face to face, although it may take place over the telephone if you are involved in telesales. *Needs Analysis* may also take place in a retail showroom or sales office where prospective customers come to you. There is no real art to conducting an effective analysis. It is all about asking the right questions to arouse emotion, called hitting the appropriate hot buttons, then listening intently to the prospect's response. Covey's book, the *7 Habits*, as mentioned earlier, has numerous chapters worthy of a read by sales people. Another of these sections in his work deals with listening, or as he puts it, *empathic listening*, and the importance of not only giving a person space, but concentrating one hundred percent on their words by looking them directly in the eye and letting them feel your sincerity. There is no stronger quality than this in the top reps – their ability to ask the right questions then just listen.

Asking questions is also known as probing, using both *Open* and *Closed Probes.*

- *Open Probes:* Questions that invite a general response, such as, "*What are the main areas related to human resources in the company that you would like to see improved?*" The sales person can take notes and interject only to clarify a point or keep the prospect on track. Open probes are often used to uncover *opportunities* to sell and these general responses may be followed by a *closed* probe.

- *Closed Probes:* These questions invoke a very brief or single word answer and they are often used to effectively convert *opportunities* to *needs*. An example of a closed probe based on a response to the open probe above, may be, "*Would you be willing to look at a solution that would improve employee turnover?*" This, of course, based upon a prospect's reply indicating that there is a problem with employee retention or morale.

- *Opportunities:* These are situations where the sales person asks an appropriate series of questions, usually through the use of open then closed probes, to uncover something that the prospect is dissatisfied with. It is important to uncover all of the opportunities that exist before trying to close the deal. In exposing opportunities, or dissatisfaction, the salesperson is making the prospect aware of a situation that exists in their organization that is generally not healthy to the bottom line, business growth potential, or possibly its competitive situation. In dealing directly with the key decision maker, usually the owner or president, it is possible to create the highest level of emotion by making the picture clear in a monetary way. At this point, the sales person may attempt a trial close, where the waters are tested to see if the prospect is warming up to purchase, however, opportunities alone are usually not enough to sell conceptual services.

- *Needs:* The all important ingredient for any sale is to convert an opportunity, or dissatisfaction, into a need which is really a prospect's willingness to do something to correct the situation. People will not buy, unless they feel a need, plain and simple. When thirsty, the situation creates a need and an individual will purchase a bottle of water or another suitable beverage. If the prospect realizes for the first time that their employee turnover is higher than industry average, the cost of recruiting, training and lost productivity may be enough for them to pay your company for a complete analysis and action plan to *improve* the situation. Note the use of benefit words, such as *improve*, and as discussed earlier in marketing planning and worth repeating, benefits satisfy needs. Can you sell on needs? You bet you can! That's the only thing you can sell on. When needs are identified and there is agreement by the prospect, it is necessary to support them with the benefits of your service. In the previous stage, a picture was painted and the prospect put in it to elevate the level of emotion. In supporting the identified needs with benefits, you are bringing them out of the picture using your solution and providing them with satisfaction. When the prospect is showing an understanding of a situation that could use improvement, and a willingness to do something about it, the process is entering the Conviction stage and the *Close* is close at hand.

The Close

This is the critical part of the presentation where the sales person moves the prospect from the conviction stage where there is a willingness to do something about an identified dissatisfaction to the Action stage where there is a commitment to utilize your solution. The close is nothing more than asking for the sale and key here, firstly, make sure that you do ask for it; and secondly, the way in which you ask for it. Prior to attempting to close the deal, you should have reviewed the analysis highlighting the prospect needs that were uncovered along with the support provided by the benefits of your offering. It is imperative to get the prospect to agree with your summary along with confirmation that your service could be beneficial as a solution to the identified problems. Once you have received the prospect's confirmation, it is time to ask for the sale. At this point, be prepared to answer objections right away. They are not a bad thing; objections are actually a natural progression and a sign that the sales process is still alive.

Asking for the sale is one of the hardest things for many sales reps to do, *(next to picking up the phone)*. It would seem unimaginable for someone to spend all of that time doing a great job prospecting, cold calling, researching the prospect, delivering a terrific presentation then leaving without a sale because there was no attempt to close, but it happens often. Asking for the sale is not difficult if you have done a good job asking the right questions during needs analysis and creating the level of emotion required by finding the hot buttons. At times the prospect will actually ask you, "*Where do I sign?*"

Figure 2-9   BENEFIT WORDS

Using the example of selling human resources services to a small or medium size business, here are some potential benefit words that may be considered to support needs that are uncovered during the probing stages: reduce employee turnover; improve profitability; increase employee productivity; make better hiring decisions; protect your investment. Note that these words strike at the bottom line – an area that business owners, the primary decision makers, can relate to.

Closing Methods

There are many ways to ask for the sale. The most obvious would be:

"*How many would you like?*"

"*When would you like to get started?*"

In a retail showroom setting the obvious would be, "*How would you like to pay?*"

When dealing with conceptual services and contracts, try to avoid discussing payment until you have a firm commitment to buy. Discuss the price in terms of investment and not cost. It will be a tax deductible expense; however, talking in terms of return on investment is very important. If your business utilizes contracts, as many service providers do, be sure to have one with you and ready at the close. The most direct way to close is to present the contract to the prospect with your pen saying, "*I just need your signature here and we can get started.*" This will certainly test the prospect's commitment to buy and bring any objections front and center. Some other closing methods to try before asking for the signature may include:

"*Would you like me to use the information on your business card for the contract?*"

"*When should we schedule the first meeting.*"

"Who else will I be working with in the company?"

Create a list of appropriate closing lines and techniques suited to your industry type.

Handling Objections

Objections are a natural part of the sales process. Keep in mind the psychology of selling – *people will naturally resist the sales process.* Following the statement or method you use to close the deal, wait patiently for the prospect to make the next move. This is where silence is golden and if you break it first it may be time to exit. The prospect's response will either be to sign your contract, ask for clarification, or make an objection to purchasing the product or service. There are several types of common objections and some are easier to handle than others. It is important to ask the appropriate questions to uncover and deal with the objection. The initial objection may only be masking an underlying objection and if that is not determined, a sale is unlikely. When dealing with objections, never contradict the prospect's statement by saying, *"No. You're wrong."* Any type of contradiction will lead to friction and impede a sale. Listen carefully to the prospect without interrupting then acknowledge their position by saying, *"Good Point."* Then ask them a question relating back to your analysis where they agreed with a need and the supporting benefit. Methods of dealing with common objections are listed below.

- *Price:* Price is often an underlying objection. The way to deal with this objection is to speak in terms of investment and, if possible, use illustrations of the return on investment by giving examples. In the case of the HR consultant, the cost of recruiting, training, lost productivity, and fines for non-compliance with government regulations are huge compared with your fee for service. It is all about value.

- *Skepticism:* This is probably the easiest objection to deal with, if you are prepared. Skeptical prospects do not believe your claims of return on investment or that your solution can fix their problem. One of the sales tools that will be described later is the *portfolio* which carries testimonials from existing satisfied customers, also known as proof source material. Testimonials will generally be in the form of a letter from a pleased customer describing your company, or you, in terms of the solution that satisfied their company objectives. If necessary, provide the prospect with phone numbers for verification. Proof sources may include certification of specialization, published material about your business, proof of bonding or insurance, and samples of actual work completed if available.

- *Indifference:* This is the toughest objection to overcome. Indifference means that the prospect has a "*So, big deal!*" opinion of your solution. This attitude is a result of a poor analysis where the right probes were not made, opportunities and needs were not exposed and no emotion was generated. The only way to deal with indifference is to start over using the proper probing and listening techniques. It is unlikely that the prospect will permit you to correct your mistake on their clock so do your best to get to the *unconsciously competent* stage of selling skills as soon as possible.

- *Stalling:* It is very common for prospects to say, "*Let me think about it.*" Another line may be, "*Call me next week.*" This means that there is no sense of urgency, generally because you have not generated enough emotion. However, it could be that the prospect did not have a truly identifiable need for your service. In this case, a sale will be difficult and leaving them with your contact information may be the best you can do. In the case where you have uncovered a definite need, there is a solid case for them to purchase now, therefore a new sense of urgency must be created. Review the parts of the analysis where the prospect confirmed a need and the benefits used to support it along with their agreement, then try closing again. It is obviously not always possible to close a deal during the first meeting. (If you are selling a commercial aircraft it may take months). The truth about most small business services is that once you leave the room, the prospect will start thinking more about the expense and less about the benefit unless they have committed to your solution by signing a contract.

There are some tactics that can be used to attempt a close or at least keep the sales process alive. Here are some scenarios using our HR consultant again.

Scenario 1 – Meeting with Influencer: Earlier we discussed the business buying hierarchy and the importance of meeting with the top decision maker, usually the owner or president. In this scenario our presenter met with the office manager to discuss HR services. After the presentation a close was attempted and the prospect (influencer) said the contract had to be presented to the owner. In this scenario, consider the sale dead unless you are prepared to go over the manager's head and start over with the top decision maker.

Scenario 2a – Meeting with Decision Maker - Closing: In this scenario you have met with the owner or president and want to go the extra distance to get the sale. This scenario requires the character of a strong closer and is not suggested for everyone unless you are a good judge of character, have the ability to ask tough but pertinent questions, and know when to back off. Try these techniques as a last ditch effort to close:

"I can leave you some information (or call you in a week) but what will happen to it tomorrow and the next day as it gets compressed in your paper tray? Wouldn't it be better to get this protection started now before you get too busy and forget about the benefits?"

"It has been my experience of the companies that I visited with similar circumstances that a solution was seldom implemented after I left."

"Why don't we get started with the analysis portion of the solution and look at the action plan later?"

"Wouldn't you agree that you have little to lose and much to gain by giving this solution a try?"

Note the use of questions whenever possible. Try to avoid making statements as they have a tendency to cause people to become defensive. Early in my sales career when I was selling life insurance products, I was a top producer in the country because I believed in the product and I was a strong closer. It was difficult enough to cold call for appointments, so I certainly wasn't going to easily give up on a sale if I knew the prospect had a genuine need, and keep in mind, if I didn't sell, I didn't get paid. Remember the old poverty motivator for the self employed. In the life insurance business, sales reps were generally selling replacement income to young families. In the event of the death of the primary bread winner, there was usually just company life insurance which would not provide a satisfactory monthly income to help the surviving spouse raise and educate the children. Often this primary bread winner would say they really didn't think it was needed and instead of giving up on the sale, because I knew they did need it, I would on occasion use this line. *"You have a beautiful home and I can see from the photos that your two sons enjoy playing hockey, which is a very expensive sport. We have looked at the income that would be available to the family if you suffer an untimely early death and you agreed that the numbers didn't add up. Would your wife be forced to marry someone she didn't really love to keep the family in this lifestyle?"* Now this sounds very harsh, but there was usually a sale, and no one got angry except for the non-bread winning spouse for the lack of income protection. Without a firm closing tactic, I would have been out a sale, but more importantly; this family would have been without adequate protection.

During weekly sales meetings in my management days, all of the reps would share their experiences from the previous week. There may be some role play to fine tune cold calling or closing skills and they would occasionally be reminded of an analogy that I enjoyed using on the utilization of firm closes. I compared the sales rep to a major league baseball pitcher facing a good batter near the end of the season. The batter hugs the plate making it hard for the pitcher to throw a strike without giving up a home run. The only recourse is to give up the home run (*walk away from the sale*) or throw a brush back pitch, possibly beaning the batter, and striking him out (*making the sale*). In the latter instance, the pitcher gets a renewed contract (*the sales person keeps their job*).

> <u>*Scenario 2b – Meeting with Decision Maker – Not Closing:*</u> In this scenario you have met with the owner or president and everything has been done unsuccessfully to secure a sale and you are not prepared to use the strong close, possibly because of the prospect's character, or your own. In this case, there is no use continuing but you don't want to lose the sale. There are some things you can do to keep the sale alive:
>
> o   Complete a contract and leave it with the prospect unsigned.
>
> o   Ask the prospect to get out their day timer, then request an appointment to return and sign the contract. This is the next best scenario as simply agreeing to touch base in a week to arrange an appointment will likely not happen.
>
> o   If the solution involves some complexity, it may be necessary to prepare a detailed proposal. A proposal may also be required if the prospect is planning to get a competitive bid.
>
> o   If there is a competitive bid, it is always advantageous to present your proposal last. If your proposal will not be presented last, ask

the prospect to consult with you to be sure that they are comparing apples with apples before making a decision. Try to learn the name of the company you are competing against and be sure to write your advantage into the proposal. Do not bad mouth the competition under any circumstance as this will alienate your prospective customer. It is fine to stress your competitive advantage but speak more on positives than negatives.

The Proposal

Similar to the contract, the proposal will leave no questions unanswered about the project, the time necessary to complete it, and the cost. The proposal must be well written using a word processor utilizing proper grammar and spelling. The document is also a testament to your professionalism. It should include a cover sheet, table of contents and the following sections:

- *Summary of the Prospect's Situation:* This will let the prospect know that you understand their position and the goals that they would like to achieve.

- *Scope of Work:* Describe the work to be done but don't give away any secrets that the competition can use if you lose the bid. Include your company expertise and competitive advantage. If the project is very large and a number of personnel will be utilized, put the company information and personnel credentials in a separate section.

- *Time Frame:* List the proposed start and completion dates for each phase and the implementation date if applicable.

- Investment: List the total cost along with a breakdown showing down payment and progress payments. If possible, show the return.

- *Delivery:* Preferably in person after competitive bids.

- *Technology:* Should match or exceed that of the competition. If a competitive proposal is delivered to the prospect as a PowerPoint presentation with a laptop and projector, you should match the technology if possible.

2.11.5 Sales Tools

As described earlier, if your operation sells products or services primarily to consumers, the promotion budget will be substantial and dedicated almost entirely to advertising. The number one way to promote a business that sells to other businesses is through personal selling. Therefore, the budget for this type of enterprise will primarily be aimed at supplying effective sales tools for you or your team.

- *The Business Card:* Undoubtedly, this is the number one tool that you will carry with you everywhere you go. Keep a supply in your notebook case; in your wallet; in your car; even your golf bag. Never be caught without business cards as you will always be networking. The card is meant to provide contact information so make sure the phone number and web site font is large enough to be read easily.

- *Presentation Binder – Portfolio:* This is your number one presentation tool. The portfolio is a collection of material that will provide a back up for everything you say. Include your customer testimonials and if applicable photos of your work as a proof source; press releases; newspaper or magazine articles; proof of professional accreditation; certificates of achievement or membership in industry associations; proof of insurance or bonding if necessary; rate sheets; product sheets with details and specifications; contracts; and any other material that support your claims. These should be compiled neatly in a professional looking binder with your logo, company name, and tag line on the cover.

- *Marketing Collateral:* Glossy folders with product information in the sleeves and a slot for a business card are ideal for a sales person to hand out. The folders must be first class (*remember image*), and the product inserts should have staggered heights for easy retrieval. Also, if one product changes, this set up requires that only one insert needs to be replaced.

- *Promotional Products:* Pens, golf balls, and other items with your name imprinted can be a good way to keep your business name in the customer's face. Ideally, the item you choose will be used frequently and if there is limited space, make sure your company web site address comes first.

- *Web Site:* The company web site can be classified as part of the promotional strategy or a function of operations. *(Web sites are covered in detail in Section 4.2)* As a part of promotion, the web site has become one of the most powerful tools the sales person can have. The prospect has instant access to high quality color Adobe .pdf format brochures that can be downloaded instantly and printed.

- *Trade Shows:* Similar to networking, trade shows are generally a function of prospecting for most companies. Sales can be made at shows, however, the show is primarily used as a place to meet new prospects, get their names in the contact management database, then have a sales person follow-up with them after the show. One of the most effective methods for collecting prospect names at a trade show is the fish bowl contest. Prospects put their business cards in the fish bowl to enter the contest and a name is drawn at the end of the show for an advertised prize that the company provides. This is a great way to collect names for the database but they may need further qualification later. Sales people at the show may qualify the names prior to card submission. Devices are also available to scan business card data directly into your PDA or contact management software.

2.11.6 Networking

Networking is an ongoing activity for any person involved in sales. Good sales people always carry a business card and are ready at the drop of a hat to give a stranger their benefit speech. Networking is actually a function of prospecting, as a sale is seldom made while actually engaging new people. A meeting is set up with the new contact at a later date where the sale is made. There are really two reasons to network.

- *Networking for Customers:* Most people will consider this to be the primary reason to network and meet new prospects. The sales person will introduce new qualified companies and people to the contact management database for the purpose of converting them to customers at a later date.

- *Networking for Referrals:* Many business owners and sales people ignore this powerful way to prospect. Instead of looking at everyone you meet as a prospective new customer, think of them in terms of a new networking center. Each established business person will have their own network of business people and that number can be quite substantial. Getting to know these individuals may lead to an invitation to become part of their circle of business acquaintances. This association can result in more referrals and the increased exposure can open many doors and introduce new opportunities to your company.

There are many places to network. The following are a few common examples:

- *Chambers of Commerce:* These organizations specialize in this area and most will have Chamber members host monthly business after hours and breakfast or lunch networking functions.

- *Industry Associations:* Most industries have associations that provide a number of benefits to member companies. In addition to providing vital information and advanced education opportunities, many member groups offer discounted insurance products and networking opportunities with other member companies. Although many attendees will be competitors, opportunities to learn and obtain referrals for sub contract work may exist.

- *Social Clubs:* Memberships in social and sports clubs can be an excellent place to network. In a golf club setting, try to play with new people on occasion as the important question is almost always asked, "*What do you do for a living?*"

Networking Dos and Don'ts

- *Do* - have a good networking (benefit) speech.
- *Do* - make as many contacts as possible during a session.
- *Do* - introduce other people into a group discussion.
- *Do* - collect business cards and enter them in to your contact manager.
- *Do* - follow up with each new contact you meet within the first week.
- *Don't* - try to make a sale while networking.
- *Don't* - monopolize one person's time as they want to meet other people.

2.11.7 Sales Force Development

As your *B2B* enterprise grows in size, so does the requirement for the owner to spend more time on administrative and operational functions. This means hiring sales people and if your company gets large enough, the establishment of a sales force with a manager to sell upscale accounts in addition to recruiting and coaching team members. There are some very important aspects of a sales force that must be understood if you are going to develop such an important coherent unit.

Development Strategy

Key areas of sales force development include:

- *Design:* This area includes determining the territorial structure then matching a customer profile with the appropriate sales type profile.

- *Recruiting:* Once you know the sales type required, an action plan for recruiting new reps can be developed.

- *Training - Compensation:* When a new rep is hired, they must be trained, coached and compensated adequately.

Territorial Structure

When you hire your first sales person, the territorial structure is very basic. This person will likely sell all company products to all prospects in all geographic areas. As your sales force grows, there is a need to keep these eager reps from stepping on each other's toes and double calling prospective customers. A larger sales force can have one of several structures.

- *Geographic Territory:* This popular structure simply assigns a specific geographic area to each sales person. The reps sell all of the company products or services to all prospects within their assigned territory only. It is important to ensure that each territory has an equitable number of qualified prospects.

- *Product:* A sales person is assigned a specific product or service to sell in all geographic areas. These reps become experts in specific product solutions that generally require a great deal of knowledge to sell, implement and service. The balance of company products and services are generally sold by the remainder of the sales force in a standard geographic territory arrangement.

- *Customer:* This sales person is specialized in certain industries or customer type. It is also known as a *Vertical* structure when industry is the key factor and the account executive becomes an industry expert. Similar to the *Product* territory structure, the balance of company products and services are generally sold by the remainder of the sales force in a standard geographic territory arrangement.

Sales Type Profile

Not all sales people have the same character. There are various strengths that are suited for different customer needs and a different approach is often required.

- *Closing:* The closing type of sales person is very high in self-confidence and very positive. The glass is always half full and the presentation is their stage where they can perform their theatrics. These optimistic reps handle rejection well and they are best motivated by high commission or bonus structures, recognition and status. The *closer* always looks after number one.

- *Consultative:* This sales character type is technically competent, a good negotiator, and well suited to the preparation and delivery of detailed proposals along with follow up service. They are highly image conscious team players who are motivated by career opportunity, brand recognition and compensation.

- *Showroom:* The showroom sales type is usually very friendly and has good product knowledge. They tend to have low ambition and are motivated by company image, vacation, benefits, hours, and company perks.

Matching Customer Profiles

During the marketing planning process, and again during the pre-prospecting phase, a profile was created of the primary customer. Prior to hiring sales people, a more detailed profile is required. Check your customer profile with those listed below then match to the appropriate sales type for the purpose of adopting effective recruiting practices.

Figure 2-10   MATCHING SALES TYPE TO CUSTOMER TYPE

The customer requires an emotional appeal to stimulate the purchase. Low contact means the sale is generally made on the first visit and an extended follow up or customer service period is not required. *B2B conceptual sales and life insurance are examples.*	**Closing**
The customer requires more technical assistance throughout the entire process from purchase and implementation to support. There is a high level of contact involved and continued customer service support after the sale. *Examples would include more high tech B2B sales.*	**Consultative**
The customer requires convenience and purchases primarily on price with a demand for product knowledge. This is often an order taking function with low contact and no follow up. *Retail and business showroom sales.*	**Showroom**

It is possible that a customer may require a closing / consultative approach and there are sales people that have characteristics common to both.

Recruiting

As I mentioned at the start of this section, good sales people are very hard to find because they are all working and making very good money. Regardless of the method chosen to recruit, a strong incentive will be required to entice a quality rep away from their good paying position at a well established company. Often younger people, right out of college, work out well because they tend to be eager and have not been influenced by bad habits or outdated methods. Once you understand your customer profile and match a sales type to it, recruiting becomes more effective. There is nothing worse than hiring the wrong sales character for your customer profile as you most often set up the recruit for failure. In addition, there is a considerable waste in company time with lost revenue and non-recoverable resources expended in recruiting and training. Prior to recruiting any employees, it is extremely important to write a detailed job description so there is no doubt regarding duties and expectations. Two common methods of recruiting sales people include:

- *Executive Search:* An agency will take your requirements and use them to find an appropriate short list of qualified individuals for you to interview. They may also try to solicit a top rep away from the competition on your behalf. In this case, be aware of any baggage they carry such as confidentiality agreements if you expect them to bring a plethora of large accounts. Fees for an executive search firm can be substantial, in the tens of thousands, or an equivalent to a large portion of the recruit's first year salary. Check to see if they offer a performance guarantee. Should the new rep not work out for any reason within the first six months or other specified period, there may be a pro-rated charge back.

- *In-House:* Purchase classified ad space that is large enough to stand out and include your minimum requirements. Conduct your own screening and interviews. Candidate referrals from reliable sources may also be considered for the position. Should you decide to do your own recruiting, familiarize yourself with all applicable labor standards. As a sales manager, I conducted the company sales force recruiting in house. When a short list was drafted, candidates were required to sell a judging panel our own company products after studying the benefits and features. It worked extremely well to see if they actually had the skills that were listed on the resume.

Training – Coaching and Compensating

It is very difficult in a competitive environment to locate and hire good people. Once they are on board, it is your responsibility as an employer to give your new sales person appropriate training to help ensure success and to provide a level of compensation that will keep productive people from leaving the team. This principle actually applies to all employees.

- *Training:* Without the proper training, you are throwing a new rep to the wolves, especially if they are new to sales and need to learn the basic skills in addition to product knowledge. A brand new sales person with good training will need three to six months to reach a level where they can produce steady results. An experienced sales person may require up to three months as their learning curve above all involves absorbing product knowledge. Training methods include:

o *Manuals:* Take the time to write a detailed job description. This will be used in recruiting ads and employee handbooks or training manuals. This should leave no doubt in the sales rep's mind as to the expectations the company has including hours of work, call and appointment activity levels, monthly performance expectations, compensation and benefits. Basically, leave no questions unanswered. A training manual will also include product or service information outlining benefits and features that differentiate from the competition along with any tried and true sales methods unique to the industry and the appropriate paper-trail or software usage required in the sales process.

o *Classroom:* There are many formal training methods available for learning or improving sales skills. These include classroom courses offered by some training organizations in major centers, on-line or video training, books and training manuals, and weekly or monthly training sessions in your own facility. Consider offering your reps an allowance to attend a sales training center. The investment to a third party that has the experience and specialization to instruct in sales skills can provide a tremendous return. Try teaching a family member to drive an automobile – some people can do it but many send them to a driving school where results are usually better.

o *Sales Meetings:* Regular meetings for the sales reps are a great idea, and very necessary, but only if they are conducted properly. The sessions should take place at a time that is not prime for selling and all reps are available. Meetings should have a structure and consistency, offer a learning experience for all to share and an opportunity for each individual to grow by taking turns in moderating the meeting. My meetings were scheduled for Monday mornings to give everyone a kick start to the week. Company or industry news was presented first followed by the *good – bad – and ugly* recount from all reps covering their previous week experiences for all to share and offer advice. It would finish with a role playing session where all the reps helped an individual with a tough close or objection. In essence, the meeting was also a valuable training and knowledge sharing opportunity for the new recruit and all participants.

o *Mentoring:* Formal training and sales meetings are good for theory but nothing beats true experience. Before sending your rookie rep out on the road, have them spend a few days with an experienced sales pro if possible. If not, let them tag along with you for cold calls and visits to prospective and existing clients to learn the ropes. Reverse the roles and observe while they give it a try. Review the performance afterward providing constructive criticism and more role play. After they go solo, track their stats and ratios for improvement and take an occasional trip on the road with them. As their sales grow, so should their autonomy.

• *Coaching:* Inspiring and motivating your sales reps is an ongoing process. Managers have become coaches over the past few decades, a dramatic improvement over the previous outdated autocratic styles. Managing is the process of administering company policy to achieve organizational objectives. Coaching is all about people and helping them to become the best that they can be. Back to the 80 : 20 rule and the top performing reps in the twenty percentile that are doing eighty percent of the production. These people are highly motivated to start with and generally only need encouragement, recognition when deserved and an appropriate level of autonomy. The eighty percent will demand more of your time and most will need serious coaching to elevate self-confidence and make their numbers. Build on strengths and learn from mistakes. Much is written on the subject of coaching and employee relations, a subject well worth studying for the owner of any business that has employees.

• *Compensation:* Good sales people are motivated by recognition and money. If you are not prepared to pay an above average remuneration, it will be impossible to attract a top candidate. The offer of straight commission in order to eliminate the need to pay regular salary expenses does not attract star performers. People new to sales will generally starve on straight commission as will sales people who are lazy or lacking in fundamental skills. A big mistake made by many small business owners is to hire an individual as a contractor to avoid paying salary expenses such as taxes and benefits. It is not a mistake to hire a sales agent or someone who is a bona fide contractor willing to add your products or services to their portfolio. Let's assume, however, that you are a typical small business ready to add a sales person to the company.

In order to locate a good person to join your small business in a sales role, certain guarantees will be required. Although high commission and a recognized brand can attract some top performers, the offer of a base salary plus commission or bonus is a proven way to keep your fax machine or inbox busy with resumes. Once you have determined that company growth can substantiate the addition of a new employee, determine what the cost of that person will be and make certain that you factor in benefits including the employer portion of their income deductions, car or mileage allowances, cell phone and other expenses. Your break-even point with the new employee will help you to determine the starting point for their quota and bonus levels. *(See the Finance section for information on costs and break-even.)*

The most effective way to pay an employee is with a base salary and performance based incentives. It is also the fairest way to ensure that the best are rewarded and stay motivated. Those employees who fail to earn incentives have no one to blame but themselves so long as they are provided with equal opportunities to learn and perform. Unfortunately with many company positions that are clerical in nature, it is difficult to measure performance in a quantitative way. Since sales are totally driven by numbers, it is relatively easy to measure individual and team results for the purpose of determining bonus levels. Keep in mind that it may take three to six months for a new rep to get up to speed if they are provided with appropriate training and support. The learning curve should be a probationary period in case they don't work out. You will know within three months if the new hire is an asset or a high maintenance liability.

2.12 Customer Service

Service and retention strategies are often overlooked by companies of all sizes. It is a fact that the cost to bring a new customer on board is much higher than it is to up sell an existing one. Most are lost due to poor service and the beneficiary of this costly mistake is always the competition. There are many negative consequences associated with a lost customer, including: the loss of residual revenue, the added customers you can potentially bring on board from their referrals and the creation of bad publicity that can take years to reverse. Levels of customer service seem to have fluctuated with economic cycles over the past few decades. The 1980s were a boom time in the economy and many businesses got very fat. Unfortunately many also got complacent and customer service suffered. The recession of the early nineties witnessed many business failures, mergers and acquisitions with larger, stronger, customer driven companies emerging into the next period of economic growth. Many new companies emerged and unfortunately as these businesses get portly through renewed economic prosperity, service again became lean. The companies that maintain high levels of customer service will generally emerge as the strongest players out of every economic downturn.

Customer service is more than just a couple of words that a company puts on their brochure or mission statement. It is part of the corporate culture and a way of doing business that all employees, regardless of position, must believe in. It is evident in companies where all contact with customers is met with a friendly disposition and sincere attention to needs. It means unconsciously going the extra distance in problem solving to provide solutions and value that will not only make the client want to come back repeatedly, but also encourage them to refer their friends and associates to do business with you. There are some great service driven companies – unfortunately they are becoming harder to find. One such company that comes to mind is *The Home Depot*. I have always found their associates in most stores to be friendly, and in accordance with corporate policy, they actually seem to enjoy meeting customers and assisting until their needs are met. At the other end of the spectrum, the poorest customer service I now encounter is at fast food outlets – all of them. With few exceptions, these employees seldom make eye contact, most don't smile and I have performed a little test which convinced me that they are almost all robotic and don't listen. Whenever I order, I will say very clearly at the end, "*Make that to go please.*" After keying in the order, they will always say, without looking up, "*Is that for here or to go?*" Try it sometime then make sure your employees don't act the same way with your customers.

Customer Satisfaction Surveys

How will you know if your customers are not satisfied with your service? For many businesses, it is when they start buying from the competition, and then it is too late. Assuming that your customers are satisfied is dangerous. Markets are very turbulent and continually changing along with customer needs. The company that responds to those changes in the most efficient and timely fashion can make loyalty a thing of the past at your expense. The proven effective method for determining satisfaction levels and understanding changing customer needs is through the survey, either formal or informal.

- *Formal Surveys:* The contact management database is the tool that marketers use to generate and deliver customer surveys. They can be sent by mail; however, Email is preferable as the message will provide a link to a special page that can be created on the company web site. The most honest answers result from anonymity. The most important questions that must be answered are as follows:

  o How would you rate the level of service we provide?
     Excellent – Good – Fair – Poor

  o What do you like about us?

  o What can we do to improve?

  Retail outlets can also provide ballots in the store for existing and new customers to submit. For new customers, these questionnaires on the ballots should include valuable contact, demographic, and intention to buy information thus producing very rich additions to the marketing database.

- *Informal Surveys:* In lieu of conducting formal surveys, it is possible to get direct feedback from customers. You must brief your employees to always ask the same questions and ask for honest answers. Unfortunately, most people are not willing to provide negative feedback in person.

Other questions to consider would be industry related and relevant to determining if customer needs are changing and in which way. It is important to conduct these surveys on a yearly basis and analyze the information objectively. The results should affirm your strengths and expose your weaknesses. Planning and action tactics can then be implemented to leverage the strengths, eliminate the weaknesses, and change the way you do business if necessary to keep your customers from going elsewhere.

Methods to Improve Customer Service

- *Employee Education:* Great customer service starts at the front line. Provide training sessions, access to seminars, and impress on all staff members the advantages that satisfied customers have for all stakeholders. Create a reward program for employees who generate good customer feedback by displaying service awards on a wall of fame and running contests with prizes geared to the winning employee's personal interests. Staff will always be on their best behavior in your presence. Some companies utilize *secret shoppers* to provide management with feedback on good and poor service practices. Employee contact with customers over the phone should not be overlooked for appropriate etiquette. Those staff members with Email access must adhere to Internet etiquette protocols: never use all caps when composing messages as this is considered shouting, use upper and lower case properly, return all correspondence promptly, watch the tone in the message and proof the draft before sending. Once a piece of electronic mail has been sent there is no chance for retrieval. The message can be forwarded by a recipient to multiple addresses and it may never disappear.

- *Business Culture:* Treating employees with respect and instilling in them a *buy-in* to the advantages of great customer service can be contagious. These positive feelings will be passed on to customers and all other company stakeholders.

- *Retention Strategy:* Include customer service in your planning by developing a retention strategy. This should include employee input as they probably know the customer best and what it may take to retain their business. In a *B2B* enterprise, it is important to count your eggs and make sure they are not all in the same basket. Look at your ten largest customers and the percentage of revenue they account for. Here comes the 80 : 20 rule again. Your largest customers will need personal contact on a more frequent basis while a majority of smaller clients may be satisfied with telephone service. Think of ways to encourage referrals. The use of patronage awards, such as discounts and coupons, is widely utilized. Finally, stay on top of the competition's service methods and when it comes to customer needs, don't assume anything. (*This topic is covered again in Section 4.4 – Contingency Planning*).

Section 3:

finance

Taking Care of Business

3.1 Financial Management

As discussed in the Introduction, any business can be divided into three distinct modules for the purpose of business planning or process analysis. This section deals with the ***Financial Module*** which covers all aspects of money management and measurement. These include bookkeeping, regulatory compliance, sales forecasting, cash flow forecasting, budgeting and capital procurement.

Finance relates to money, therefore *Financial Management* relates to how money is managed. Some of the important goals of *Financial Management* include:

- *Profitability:* Ensuring that revenue exceeds expenses.

- *Growth:* Setting goals and implementing plans to grow the business in both revenue and profitability.

- *Liquidity:* Maintaining an adequate level of liquid assets at any given time to meet obligations.

- *Stability:* Balancing short and long-term debt as well as having access to needed capital.

Poor financial management is the number one reason why businesses fail. The following is a list of some of the most common ways that businesses fail because of poor financial management.

- *Underfunding:* Most new small businesses are underfunded. This often results in the burden of excessive debt and the associated high interest payments which limit the amount of available working capital. Often the capital raised is inadequate to fund effective operational and marketing requirements with the consequence that revenues are lower than expected.

- *Over spending:* Many entrepreneurs are guilty of this and often they are unaware that there is a problem until it is too late. Some examples include growing too large too quick, extravagant office or production space with expensive re-design, and luxury vehicle leases. These are fixed costs that must be paid every month regardless of revenue.

- *Spending taxes collected:* Believe it or not, this is more common than you may realize. Many small business owners collect income and / or sales taxes and the money goes into the company current banking account where it is often utilized as working capital. At the end of the quarter, or other designated fiscal reporting period, the government's money is not available resulting in a mad scramble to secure the funds by raising company debt.

- *Failure to remit income tax:* This is most common in sole proprietorships versus corporations. In a sole proprietorship, the revenue of the company is also the income of the owner. Personal income tax must be paid on all but the portion that can be written off as legitimate business expenses. Unless tax installments or a regular salary with deductions are made, a business owner can be in quite a bind the next year to raise thousands of dollars in taxes owing to the government.

3.2 Bookkeeping Basics

A business is similar to home finances where there is a simple rule for survival and growth: ***Income must exceed expenses!***

(There may be brief, <u>planned</u> periods of growth when expenses will exceed income.)

The backbone of the financial module is the bookkeeping system. A good set of books is imperative for many reasons such as assisting in regulatory compliance and providing the basis for proper yearend financial statements. Most importantly, the reports allow the business owner to analyze the financial health of the organization and measure results by comparing actual numbers against previously set goals. The saying that follows was used in the chapter on *Personal Selling* and rings true in many other areas of business – none more obvious than in finance:

> **"If you can't measure it – you can't manage it!"**

Technology has made bookkeeping much easier with small business software packages like *Quick Books Pro* or *Simply Accounting*. These applications have good tutorials and sample companies to practice on, however, there is a learning curve. It may be more economical to outsource a bookkeeper for your weekly postings if you do not have a staff member qualified. Your time can be better spent doing what you do best. The important point here is that you do maintain a good current set of books at all times. As a business principle, it is also important that you have a basic understanding of the bookkeeping process so you know where the numbers are coming from and what they mean. The more you can learn about all aspects of business, the stronger you will be as an entrepreneur and manager. Most small businesses require the services of an accountant to prepare their company and personal tax returns along with yearend adjustments for your enterprise. These professionals are tax experts and their yearly fee can be reduced considerably if you provide them with a good set of books to work with. A clean set of company books is a must for any business as it provides the owners / managers with timely statements to measure the financial health of the enterprise. An accountant can also save you a great deal of money in taxes and a tax audit will run much smoother if you are selected for scrutiny.

Chart of Accounts

A set of company books is based on a *Chart of Accounts* in the *General Ledger*. Small business accounting software packages have sample company templates that can be used to set up a new set of books. There are templates for service, retail or manufacturing based companies and all you need to do is change the contents in the *Chart of Accounts* to suit your business. This can be easily done by deleting those accounts that you won't use and adding those you will use.

An accountant can help you to identify the accounts that are necessary for your particular business requirements. Each account has a name and a number. They are positioned in one of five sections identified by the account number that is assigned to them. Figures from the first three sections are used to create the *Balance Sheet* and those from the last two sections comprise the *Income Statement*.

- *Asset Accounts* are the first set and all of these account numbers begin with the number one. The first account in this section is likely your bank and the identifier could be 105 or 1010. This is your preference. The next account could be your receivables with an assigned number of 110 or 1020. Large companies with numerous accounts and sub-accounts will utilize more digits. The only rule is the correct first number for a particular section and no duplication is permitted.

  Assets are divided into three types:

  o *Current Assets* – those which can be converted to cash quickly. These would include bank accounts and receivables.

  o *Inventory Assets*

  o *Capital Assets* – of which there are several classes. These would include vehicles, equipment, computer hardware / software and buildings. Capital assets are amortized with varying amounts of annual depreciation.

- *Liability Accounts* comprise the second set and all of these accounts begin with the number two. The first account in this section could be your *Accounts Payable* with an identifier of 205 or 2010. Again, your preference.

  Liabilities are divided into two types:

  o *Current Liabilities* – those accounts which generally must be paid within 30 to 90 days. These would include your supplier payables, credit card balances, taxes and benefits payable from payroll and sales taxes collected that must be remitted, generally each quarter.

  o *Long Term Liabilities* – are loans. This includes any funds forwarded to or drawn by the owner as a shareholder loan.

- *Equity Accounts* comprise the third section of the *Chart* and these include the share capital accounts and an account for current earnings as well as one for retained earnings carried over from the previous fiscal year. Identifiers for these accounts begin with the number three.

- *Revenue Accounts* make up the fourth section. These accounts will itemize all areas of revenue or income. Some examples may be account 410 for product one, 420 for product two and 450 for service revenue. If you are selling a number of different products, it is necessary to assign a different account and number to each one in order to track margins and identify sales stars and dogs. If you feel there are too many items to justify individual identifiers, try to group products that are similar.

- *Expense Accounts* are the fifth section in the *Chart of Accounts*. There are two types of expenses that will be tracked, all starting in the 500 or 5000 series.

  o *Direct Costs* – are also known as *Variable Costs* or *Cost of Goods*. These expenses include raw materials, packaging, rentals for projects, commission on sales, subcontractors and any other cost that is directly related to the production of a product or delivery of a service. They are also known as *Variable Costs* because they are expected to increase as sales increase. These costs are used to determine *Gross Profit* and *Gross Margins*. (*See Section 3.4 for more detail on this important topic.*)

  o *General or Administration Costs* – are also known as *Fixed Costs* because they are the same each month. These include rent, employee salaries, insurance, office supplies, advertising and other expenses that remain the same each month.

Figure 3-1   SAMPLE CHART OF ACCOUNTS - SIMPLIFIED

105	Bank - Current Account
110	Accounts Receivable
120	Prepaid Expenses
150	Inventory Product 1
155	Inventory Product 2
180	Equipment
185	Accum. Amort. Equipment
210	Accounts Payable
240	Income Tax Payable
260	Sales Tax Payable
280	Shareholder Loan Payable
290	Bank Loan Payable
320	Common Shares
360	Retained Earnings
420	Revenue Product 1
440	Revenue Product 2
505	Materials Product 1
510	Materials Product 2
530	Accounting and Legal Fees
531	Membership and Association Fees
540	Postage and Courier
545	Office Supplies
550	Advertising
560	Salary
565	Rent
570	Automobile
580	Telephone
590	Utilities

Figure 3-1 illustrates a very simplified Chart of Accounts. There are many more accounts that your accountant can recommend for your business. During a bookkeeping session, entries will be posted to the various accounts allowing reports to be printed when required.

Period Ending Reports

As a business owner, you will need to understand the financial statements your accounting software can provide – how to read them and knowing where the numbers originate. Certain reports should be generated at the end of each accounting period to satisfy government regulations in addition to the *Balance Sheet* and *Income Statement*:

- <u>Month End</u>

  o Federal payroll source deduction remittances.

  o Worker's compensation and other fees payable.

- <u>*Quarter End*</u> (Calendar quarters end Mar. 31st, Jun. 30th, Sep. 30th and Dec. 31st .)

  o Sales tax remittance. (For each level of government)

- <u>*Fiscal Year End*</u> - a complete set of books ready for your accountant who will examine the records then provide yearend adjustments, accurate financial statements for the business, and tax returns for all levels of government.

Note:

The onus is on the business owner to know the applicable reporting requirements and make all required remittances. Consult with your accountant for advice if you're not sure.

3.3 Understanding Financial Statements

It is surprising the number of business owners who do not understand financial statements. Where the numbers come from, what they mean and what they are used for all play a key role in the comprehension of this vital business information. Prior to yearend, large publicly traded businesses set budgets for the next year. This is done to satisfy shareholder requirements for sound financial management. More small to medium size businesses should be engaging in the practice of setting financial objectives then measuring actual results. The measuring is accomplished by generating monthly, quarterly and yearly reports from the accounting software. The two financials that will be the focus of our attention are the *Balance Sheet* and the *Income Statement*.

3.3.1 Balance Sheet

The *Balance Sheet* (Fig. 3-2) is simply a snap-shot of the business liquidity at any given time. It shows how much you own, how much you owe and the equity. It utilizes information from the first three sections of the *Chart of Accounts: Assets, Liabilities and Equity*. From the balance sheet a determination of the company's net worth can be established, similar to your own personal finances, by subtracting *Liabilities* from *Assets*. The formula that makes this report balance is Assets = Liabilities + Equity. It is also used to determine key business financial ratios in established companies.

Key Financial Ratios

The following ratios are often used by bankers and other financiers when companies seek capitalization. Most are taken directly from the *Balance Sheet*. These ratios are not really *Need to Know* for most business owners, but they are *Nice to Know*.

- *Current Ratio:* This is one of the best ways to measure a company's financial health as the *Current Ratio* reveals if there are sufficient current assets to meet current debts with a margin of safety for possible losses.

  CURRENT RATIO = Current Assets / Current Liabilities

  Example: If Current Assets are $150,000 and the Current Liabilities are $100,000 then the Current Ratio = **1.5** The optimal *Current Ratio* for most businesses is 2.0 or greater, however, comparison to industry average is required.

- *Debt / Equity Ratio:* Measures business capital structure and indicates a company's ability to carry debt.

  DEBT / EQUITY = Total Liabilities / Total Equity

  Example: If Total Liabilities are $70,000 and the Total Equity is $90,000 then the Debt / Equity Ratio = **.78** A lender's judgment about this ratio being acceptable depends on industry averages.

- *Return on Investment (ROI):* A measurement of investment profitability.

  ROI = Net Profit (After Tax) / Total Assets

  Example: If Total Assets are $250,000 and the Net Profit is $50,000 then the Return on Investment = **.2 or 20%** The goal is to obtain the highest Net Profit for the smallest possible investment. ROI can be used for industry comparison, investment decisions, and measures of efficiency or profitability.

- *Inventory Turnover:* This ratio is extremely important for retailers to understand. There are several formulas and a large amount of information is available on the Internet. Conduct a search with the keywords inventory turnover.

Note: *Break-Even* and *Days Sales Outstanding* are explained in section 3.4.

Figure 3-2	BALANCE SHEET SIMPLIFIED		
ASSETS			
CURRENT ASSETS			
Bank - Current Account		XXXXX	
Accounts Receivable		XXXXX	
Prepaid Expenses		XXXXX	
Inventory Product 1	XXXXX		
Inventory Product 2	XXXXX		
Total Inventory		XXXXX	
TOTAL CURRENT ASSETS			XXXXX
CAPITAL ASSETS			
Vehicles	XXXXX		
Accum. Amortization Vehicles	XXXXX		
Vehicles Net		XXXXX	
Equipment	XXXXX		
Accum Amortization Equipment	XXXXX		
Equipment Net		XXXXX	
TOTAL CAPITAL ASSETS			XXXXX
TOTAL ASSETS			XXXXX
LIABILITIES			
CURRENT LIABILITIES			
Accounts Payable		XXXXX	
Employee Taxes Payable		XXXXX	
Taxes Collected On Sales		XXXXX	
Corporate Taxes Payable		XXXXX	
TOTAL CURRENT LIABILITIES			XXXXX
LONG TERM LIABILITIES			
Shareholder loan		XXXXX	
Bank loan		XXXXX	
TOTAL LONG TERM LIABILITIES			XXXXX
TOTAL LIABILITIES			XXXXX
EQUITY			
Common Shares		XXXXX	
Retained Earnings		XXXXX	
Current Earnings		XXXXX	
TOTAL EQUITY			XXXXX
LIABILITIES AND EQUITY			XXXXX

XXXXX =Your $$ input

Figure 3-2 is a typical Balance Sheet as it would be generated by your accounting software. It is a snapshot of the business finances at any specified time using the information from the Assets, Liabilities, and Equity sections. This sample is very basic and is missing many typical accounts.

3.3.2 Income Statement

The *Income Statement (Fig. 3-3)*, also known as the *Profit and Loss Statement*, is a measurement of *Revenue, Expenses, and Profits (Losses)* over a specified period of time. The time frame is generally a single month, quarter or fiscal year. The *Income Statement* reveals many important financial factors. These actual numbers will be used for comparison against projected numbers in the budget, hopefully created before fiscal yearend for the next one or two years. The budget is actually a *Profit and Loss* projection plotted on a spreadsheet. *(See section 3.4 on page 174 – Setting Goals and Measuring Results.)* In addition to providing details on all sources of revenue, the *Income Statement* lists the cost of goods and detailed operating expenses. *There is a Profit and Loss worksheet in MS Excel 97 – 2003 format available with this book. The template is fully formatted and complete with formulas. It can be customized to suit your business by adding rows that are required and deleting rows that are not necessary. See the Resources section near the end of the book for more information.*

The first section of the *Income Statement* is *Revenue* or *Income*. Keep in mind that these figures are generated from individual journal accounts in the 4th section of your *Chart of Accounts*. It is important to track the revenue from each major product line or service to determine which offerings are the most profitable. These can be charted after the fact using your spreadsheet software to determine which ones are trending up or down over time. The individual product or service revenue accounts must be created in the *Chart of Accounts* before the sales can be posted during a bookkeeping session and subsequently displayed on a report.

The next section of the statement details the *Expenses* and it is divided into two parts. The first part itemizes *Direct Costs*, also known as *Variable Costs* or *Cost of Goods* (COG). The second part of the *Expense* section details the *General* or *Administrative Costs* also known as *Fixed Costs*. It is important to understand the difference between these two expense types as they can provide valuable information regarding the company's financial well being. *COG* or *Variable Costs* fluctuate up and down in a direct relationship with sales. These costs include inventory, raw materials, production, packaging, warehousing, shipping, sales commission, sub-contract fees, etc. As a company sells more products or delivers more services, these expenses rise accordingly. Subtracting the *COG* from *Revenue* determines the *Gross Profit* and dividing this number by the revenue provides the *Gross Profit Margin* in a percentage of sales. Unfortunately, most small business accounting programs do not show *Gross Profit*. Thus, *Profit Margins* must be calculated by transferring information from the *Income Statement* to a spreadsheet. *(This important information is detailed in section 3.4 on page 174 – Setting Goals and Measuring Results)*. *Operating Expenses*, such as rent, are usually fixed for specific period of time and subtracting the total of these *Fixed Costs* from the *Gross Profit* provides the *Net Profit* or *Net Loss* before taxes.

The information presented on the *Income Statement* provides sales management with important information to compare with plan. The report also points out areas of excessive spending, and this allows financial managers to implement appropriate controls. Unfortunately, the basic small business programs do not provide the *Gross Profit* information that is vital to company growth and sustainability.

Figure 3-3   INCOME STATEMENT SIMPLIFIED   XXXXX=Your $$ input

REVENUE		
REVENUE: Sales		
Product 1	XXXXX	
Product 2	XXXXX	
TOTAL REVENUE: Sales		XXXXX
REVENUE: Services		
Service and Repair	XXXXX	
TOTAL REVENUE: Services		XXXXX
TOTAL REVENUE		XXXXX
EXPENSE		
DIRECT COSTS	XXXXX	
Materials Product 1	XXXXX	
Materials Product 2	XXXXX	
Parts - Service	XXXXX	
Freight	XXXXX	
TOTAL DIRECT COST		XXXXX
GROSS PROFIT		XXXXX
GENERAL AND ADMINISTRATION		
Accounting and Legal Fees		XXXXX
Membership Fees, Dues and Subscriptions		XXXXX
Advertising and Promotion		XXXXX
Charitable Donations		XXXXX
Postage and Courier		XXXXX
Bank Charges		XXXXX
Interest - Long Term		XXXXX
Amortization		XXXXX
Vehicle Lease Payments		XXXXX
Vehicle Expenses		XXXXX
Rent		XXXXX
Leasehold Improvements		XXXXX
Telephone		XXXXX
Utilities		XXXXX
Salaries		XXXXX
Salary Expenses		XXXXX
Training		XXXXX
Entertainment		XXXXX
Office Supplies		XXXXX
Travel Expenses: Lodging	XXXXX	
Travel Expenses: Meals	XXXXX	
Total Travel Expenses		XXXXX
TOTAL GENERAL AND ADMINISTRATION		XXXXX
NET INCOME (Before Taxes)		XXXXX

Figure 3-3 is a typical Income Statement as it would be generated by your accounting software. It shows Revenue and Expenses over a specified period of time and also indicates Net Profit. Tracking Revenue and Expenses can be as detailed as required.

3.4 Setting Goals and Measuring Results

3.4.1 Budgeting – Setting the Goals

Every year, large corporations go through a process that is dreaded by some managers, but expected by shareholders as a good business practice. Budgets in large private and public sector organizations are created for each department using sophisticated software. This compilation for the next fiscal year establishes the monetary goals necessary to meet corporate expectations. The onus is the sales department to meet revenue growth targets; the production department is responsible for wise purchasing decisions along with strategies to reduce waste and maintain quality; and every department in the company is responsible for staying within their prescribed operating expense ceiling to ensure overall profitability. Most small business owners wear many hats and the resources are most often not available for high end budgeting software. Therefore, basic user knowledge of spreadsheet software is a must if goals are to be established and measured effectively. My preference for software is *MS Excel*, however all spreadsheet programs function in a similar way. The report you will prepare to create a budget is a *Profit & Loss* projection, also known as a *pro rata Income Statement*. This report is created for startup businesses to measure feasibility and existing businesses to set goals. You can create a template from scratch yourself or use the *MS Excel* worksheet available for download with this publication. If you are creating your own template there will be fourteen columns. The first is reserved for revenue and expense category descriptions, columns two through thirteen are for the twelve months of the projection, and the last column creates a total for all figures across each row. Totals for each column appear across the bottom row of each section.

The first section of rows on the spreadsheet is reserved for *Revenue*. Monthly sales projections will be entered into each corresponding cell for each product or service. If you have correctly inserted formulas into your spreadsheet, the totals will automatically appear in the right column as the year is calculated and along the *Total Revenue* row for each month at the bottom of the section. All budgeting begins with sales. There are a number of ways to forecast sales. This is the most difficult area to project if you are a startup company. For existing businesses with a track record, there are several methods that can be used to forecast sales. The *top-down* method utilizes common techniques such as executive judgment (company executives determine sales goals) or trend projections where past sales trending may form a pattern that can be projected forward into future years. The bottom-up approach utilizes intention-to-buy surveys or the more common sales force composite method where each sales person forecasts the revenue potential for their own territory.

The next section of the *Profit & Loss* projection deals with *Direct* or *Variable Costs, also known as* the *Cost of Goods*. These costs fluctuate with and are directly related to sales. They may include inventory for resale if you are a distributor or retailer; raw materials for production; packaging; logistics of warehousing and shipping; advertising if it is built into the price; sales commission; sub contract fees; equipment rentals for a project; and direct overhead and labor cost if manufacturing process analysis is conducted. Are wages a direct cost? They may be – just put the cost to the test. Does it fluctuate up or down with revenue? An example would be a construction company where there is wage labor and the workers are paid only when there are projects available. If there is no work – then no pay – and this would be a fluctuating direct cost. In determining *Direct Costs*, you should be able to calculate how much it will cost you to produce and send to market each individual item or project. You should also know how much it will cost you directly to earn each dollar of revenue. Once you know your *Direct Costs*, this section almost falls into place automatically as sales numbers are projected. There will be a row for the total *Cost of Goods* for each month and a new row for the *Gross Profit*, which is the *Total Revenue* minus the *Total Cost of Goods*.

Add another row to analyze exactly what is happening with the company's financial health. This row is the *Gross Profit Margin*. The formula entered in this row will divide the *Gross Profit* from the preceding row by the *Total Revenue* to provide a percentage which indicates what fraction of the dollar earned remains to pay the rest of the operating expenses and allow for profit and growth. *(See Fig. 3-4)* For example, if the total revenue for one month was $14,000 and the Total Cost of Goods is $8,000, the Gross Profit is $6,000. This would mean that the Gross Profit Margin is 43% (Gross Profit / Total Revenue). Each dollar of revenue will cost 57 cents to earn leaving the company with 43 cents from each dollar to cover the Operating Expenses which form the next section of the spreadsheet.

Operating Expenses are also known as General Expenses or Administrative Costs. These are the expenses that don't go away because they are *Fixed Costs*.

They include salaries (all staff, management and the owner's regular pay) and all expenses related to them, rent and leasehold improvements, insurance, utilities, business travel and related expenses, entertainment, postage/ courier, bank charges and interest, subscriptions, professional dues and memberships, office supplies, advertising (if not included in the selling price of a product), vehicle expenses, and the list goes on. These amounts can be projected monthly in advance for a full year. For subsequent years in your projections, an inflation figure can be added to the rent or other items to cover reasonable increases. This section will be totaled and subtracted from the *Gross Profit* to provide the *Net Profit* before taxes.

In laying out the sales plan and budget on the *Profit and Loss* spreadsheet, caution should be used in certain areas. It is quite common to project unrealistic sales numbers and underestimate expenses. Sales forecasts should be slightly conservative and expenses somewhat liberal allowing for a slight margin of error in favor of maintaining profitability. Complete a *Profit & Loss* projection for at least the upcoming fiscal year if you have an existing business and for a minimum of three to five years if you are starting a new business venture.

Fig. 3-4   CALCULATING GROSS PROFIT and GROSS MARGIN

	January	February	March
Total Revenue	$14,000.00	$16,000.00	$15,000.00
Total Direct Costs	8,000.00	9,000.00	8,500.00
Gross Profit	6,000.00	7,000.00	6,500.00

(Revenue minus Direct Costs)

Gross Margin	43%	44%	43.5%

(Gross Profit / Revenue)
Gross Margin is determined by dividing Gross Profit by Total Revenue.

Budget Analysis and Verification

The first thing to do in examining the numbers is determine if the company can be profitable. This is especially important for new businesses as the *Profit & Loss* projection is a clear indicator of bottom line results and you will know very quickly if you are pricing your product or service for profitability. For existing businesses, this exercise will indicate immediately if there is a problem (red numbers on the bottom line) and you may need to sharpen the pencil on the expenses or find ways to sell more. The key figures on this report can also provide a business owner with other important pieces of information, such as the *Break-Even* point.

Break-Even

There are several ways to calculate break-even based on your selling price, variable cost and fixed costs. The simplest formula uses the *Gross Margin* calculated earlier, and referred to here as a *Contribution Value* or *CV*.

FIXED COST / CV = BREAK-EVEN

Example: Let's use the 43% profit margin from the previous page as the *CV*. If your *Fixed Costs* are $6,000 for one month, then the *Break-Even* point would be 6000/.43 = **$13,953**. If your *Gross Margin* were only 35% then the *Break-Even* would be **$17,000**. A 55% *Gross Margin* would translate to a *Break-Even* of **$10,900** each month – quite a difference! These examples clearly illustrate the dramatic impact that *Gross Margin* has on your *Break-Even* point. This simple formula works for any business, even a service business with no *Variable Costs*. In this case, the *Break-Even* point is the same as the monthly fixed costs.

Once you know where your *Break-Even* point is each month, it is possible to calculate how many days it will take to *Break-Even* by using your *Average Days Sales* and the number of days per month you are open for business. If your company's annual sales total $250,000.00, then the *Average Days Sales* are $685 (250,000 / 365). Using the figures from the example in the previous paragraph, the *Break-Even* would occur on the 21st day of the month. (<u>$13,953</u> / 685) Determine how much money your average customer spends and you can determine the number of customers required each month to *Break-Even*. The key here again, is knowing the *Gross Profit Margin*.

Another way to calculate the *Break-Even* point is to analyze the relationship between product sales, fixed costs, and variable costs. A little more complicated, this method determines the number of units that must be sold before the company becomes profitable.

BREAK-EVEN (Units) = FIXED COST / (PRICE – VARIABLE COST (*Per Unit*))

Example: Projected *Fixed Cost* is $100,000.00 for the next fiscal year. Retail *Price* per unit is $4.60 with a *Variable Cost* of $2.40 per unit.

Break-Even = 100,000 / (4.6 – 2.4) = 100,000 / 2.2 = 45,455 units.

3.4.2 Measuring Results

Financial goals have been plotted on a spreadsheet as part of the budget process for the next fiscal year. The business operations are creating actual numbers that can be printed on reports using the accounting software. Now, what's the next step? There must be a method to compare the actual results from the *Income Statement* with that on the budget, our *P&L* forecast. This method is known as a *Variance Analysis*. A business owner can look at the *Income Statement* at the end of each reporting period and compare it against the forecast on a spreadsheet, but this method can be very awkward. Most small business accounting programs do not provide a figure for *Gross Margin* or even *Gross Profit*. Therefore, the spreadsheet is the primary tool for this analysis, and there are a number of reasons. It provides a direct comparison between the actual numbers and the projected figures, plus the power of the spreadsheet allows the charting of the financial performance of a business in different graph formats. A chart, illustrated by a line or bar graph, indicates trending at a glance and setting up a chart in *MS Excel* is very easy to do. The spreadsheet also contains the key information that is missing from the *Income Statement* generated by the accounting software. The missing numbers are the *Gross Profit* and *Gross Profit Margin* – the importance of which cannot be overemphasized.

The first step is to create a new spreadsheet where month end figures can be input from the actual results. A monthly *Variance Analysis* report requires a sheet with thirty-seven columns – the first for description and three for each month. The first monthly column will have cells populated with actual numbers taken directly from the *Income Statement* generated by the software. The second column will receive the forecast numbers from the *P&L* projection and the third column of cells for each month will show the *Variance* in each category. It may take some time to set up your initial template with formulas but the time you save later will make the effort worth it. Be sure to name your template with the *Save As* function at the start of your work and keep clicking the *Save* toolbar button at regular intervals as you proceed, to crash protect your work. *(See Figure 3-5).*

Figure 3-5   VARIANCE ANALYSIS

	January Actual	January Forecast	January Variance	
Revenue 1	$14,800.00	$15,500.00	($ 700.00)	
Revenue 2	3,700.00	3,500.00	200.00	
TOTAL REVENUE	18,500.00	19,000.00	(500.00)	
Total Direct Costs	11,900.00	12,200.00	500.00	
Gross Profit	$ 6,600.00	$ 6,800.00	($ 200.00)	
	(Revenue minus Direct Costs)			
Gross Margin	35.7%	35.8%	0.1%	
	(Gross Profit / Revenue)			
ADMINISTRATION				
Advertising	$ 800.00	$ 1,100.00	$ 300.00	List all
Fixed Costs				

In Figure 3-5, plotting actual and forecast numbers enables analysis of the Variance. In this example, Revenue figures and Gross Profit are less than forecast; however, the Gross Margin is slightly better. Check the Variance for each month, quarter and year end. If it is clear that plan is not being achieved, the options are to lower sales expectations, improve margins by lowering COG (Cost of Goods / Direct Costs), or reducing Administrative / Operating expenses to ensure profitability. A Variance Analysis worksheet complete with formulas is available with this book.

The minimum amount of information that should be compared is *Total Revenue, Total Cost of Goods, Gross Profit, Gross Margin, Total Operating Expenses* and *Net Profit.* If you operate a business that is strictly service with no variable cost then your comparison will be simply revenue and operating expenses. This minimal comparison of actual to projected numbers is fine if the results meet plan. If there is a negative variance in any of the categories being compared, the actual cause of the variance may not be apparent. In order to determine the reason for a shortfall in gross or net profit, all of the expense categories must be compared. Detailed operating expense categories are also suggested to measure adherence to plan objectives.

Once there are several months of variance comparisons, a chart can be created in the form of a line or bar graph to provide an instant visual alert to any negative trending. The primary numbers to chart are *Total Sales, Gross Margin* and *Net Profit* as this will keep the graph clean, although *Total COG (Cost of Goods), Gross Profit* or any individual category can be plotted on a graph. Keep in mind that it takes several months, or at least two fiscal quarters to really gauge a trend. Many companies experience a growth in sales, sometimes rapid, yet find themselves in financial difficulties, not knowing why. Understanding the key numbers, where they come from and current trending are financial management indicators of the organization's fiscal health. I have seen a number of cases where sales growth in a business was rapid yet the company was struggling to keep their head above water. Analysis showed tremendous growth in revenue, a growth in gross profit, which was expected, but an ever increasing loss on the bottom line. The companies did not know that their gross profit margins were shrinking and eventually it would put them out of business.

This clearly illustrates the importance of measuring results. The budgeting and forecasting process provides a road to travel to the next stop; however, it is the analysis of actual results versus plan that warns if a wrong turn is taken. When a negative indicator does sound an alert then actions can be taken to correct the situation. If your sales numbers are not overstated and unachievable, yet are not being met, there are two possible remedies: Light a fire under the sales force (this may be you), and/or improve your marketing strategy and initiatives.

In the latter case, the plan should be re-written with realistic projections and although this reduces the cost of goods, there must be enough gross profit left to cover operating expenses, taxes and at least a modest profit. If operating expenses appear high then start trimming wherever possible to maintain a healthy bottom line. Let's get back to the gross profit margin. There is no real problem if this number remains constant. *(See Figure 3.6)* If the gross margin starts to decrease, it is a sign that your business could be in trouble. There are only two ways to improve the margin and increasing sales is not the answer. The first way is to raise your price. Many businesses try to compete by offering the lowest price and the result is often financial difficulty. To beat the competition on price, your company must be leaner. Lowering the cost of goods is the second method of increasing the gross profit margin. This is accomplished by shopping around for different suppliers to find a better price (be careful not to sacrifice quality); buying in larger quantities to receive discounts; or streamlining operations by introducing more efficient processes (economies of scale).

Figure 3-6   MARGIN ANALYSIS

	January	February	March	TOTAL Q1
Revenue 1	$12,800.00	$14,100.00	$15,300.00	$42,200.00
Revenue 2	1,400.00	1,550.00	2,250.00	5,200.00
TOTAL REVENUE	14,200.00	15,650.00	17,550.00	47,400.00
Total Direct Costs (COG)	8,800.00	9,900.00	11,650.00	30,350.00
Gross Profit	$ 5,400.00	$ 5,750.00	$ 5,900.00	$17,050.00
Gross Margin	38%	36.7%	33.6%	

In Figure 3-6, these amounts would represent the actual performance numbers transferred from the Income Statement. At first glance, the results look good: sales are up and the gross profit is up. However, there is a serious problem. The margin is slipping and this company will go out of business if this trend is left unchecked. The company's principles can now analyze the problem and determine why the margins were trending this way and turn it around before it is too late. The analysis could show that they were pricing the work too low, paying too much for materials, or both. Plotting a chart quickly exposes this problem.

3.5 Extending Credit and Receivables Management

One of the important considerations for business owners is determining the best way to be paid for products or services. There are a number of considerations to keep in mind.

- *Making it easy for the customer to buy:* For retailers and many service providers, this means accepting cash along with bank or credit card payments even if there is a small fee or commission payable. Personal checks are always a risky form of payment and should be avoided.

- *Competitive methods:* A competitive analysis before startup for a new company, and periodically for an existing business, should include an assessment of typical methods they accept for payment. If the major competitors accept credit card payments, it is imperative that you set up a merchant account to do the same. If they extend credit, it may be necessary for your company to offer terms. Failure to do so may drive the customers to the competition where it is more convenient to purchase goods or services.

- *Extending Credit:* B2C enterprises seldom extend credit on their own. Retailers of larger ticket items often extend credit through finance companies who then accept the risk. In many industries, *B2B* enterprises are expected to offer a variety of payment methods to remain competitive, including the extension of credit terms. Extending credit requires a strict receivables management policy to remain in business.

Bad Debt and the Bottom Line

In a sense, there are a number of businesses that are in a *catch 22* situation when it comes to offering customers credit terms. Failing to extend credit may result in lost customers, yet extending credit involves risk and possible losses. Some industries anticipate a certain amount of bad debt each year for member companies, such as .25% of annual sales as an example. Being stuck with a bad debt still hurts no matter which way you look at it, and for some companies, more than others. The financial consequences resulting from a bad debt vary depending upon the margin. A $5,000 bad debt means that a great deal of additional product must be sold in order to make up for the loss if you have a low margin. Here are a couple of instances. With a margin of 10%, you need to sell an additional $50,000 in product to cover the debt. At 25% it is $20,000 and at 100% the sales required would be equal to the debt of $5,000. If it is strictly a service business without direct costs, it is often your own time and again extra sales would equal the debt to reach break-even. Don't forget that there are still operating expenses to pay. There is no way to totally eliminate the risk involved in the extension of credit if you finance the receivables yourself. There are a number of ways to minimize the risk and it starts with a sound *Receivables Management Plan.*

Three Part Process

If your company needs to extend credit to customers, it is essential to have a *Receivables Management Plan* in place. The primary purpose of developing the plan is reducing risk. There are other reasons as well, such as improving customer service and increasing sales.

Accounts receivable management is a three phase process:

- *Credit Screening*
- *Monitoring Credit Accounts*
- *Collections*

Reducing risk is an effort that takes place in each of these phases. Before discussing the stages of the process, it is important to understand some key terms and principles.

Aged Receivables

When a company extends credit to customers, there are terms of repayment specified. Perishable items typically require repayment in less than ten days. Most products and services, however, have typical repayment terms of thirty days or one month attached to them. At the end of each accounting reporting period, as discussed earlier in this chapter, certain reports will be printed by the company bookkeeper. When a company offers credit to its customers, a list of receivables is created and an additional report must be printed each month. This document, called an *Aged Receivables* report, shows every outstanding customer invoice with an amount in each period of aging. For a company offering thirty day terms, these periods would be specified as follows:

- <u>Current:</u> *All outstanding invoices that have not reached their due date.*

- 1st period: *Those invoices that are 31 to 60 days old.*

- 2nd period: *Invoices that are aged 61 to 90 days.*

- 3rd period: *Delinquent accounts that are more than 90 days past due.*

Aged Receivables is the report that the credit department works each month when engaged in collection activities.

Liberal or Conservative Receivables Management

- *Liberal:* It is difficult for many new business owners to turn down a sale, even if it means taking a chance. The instant sale posted to accounts receivable can often cloud thoughts of a possible entry to the bad debt account months down the road. Businesses that are highly sales driven with minimal consideration to credit risk are considered liberal in their credit or accounts receivable management policy. These companies must have high margins with lower priced items to survive as losses tend to be high and a large percentage of receivables would be in the 2nd or 3rd period of aging.

- *Conservative:* Many companies, often those with higher priced products or lower margins also have a low tolerance for risk. The high negative impact on the bottom line forces many of these businesses to adopt a very conservative approach to extending credit. Extensive up front credit screening may include credit report analysis, and this is only the start for a conservative credit grantor. Their receivables management process demands strict adherence to terms and accounts are monitored closely with credit holds when an invoice ages to the 1st period. Credit limits often rise as customers prove their worthiness.

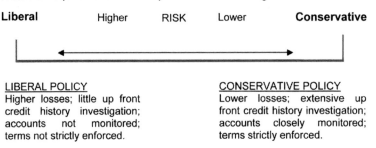

Figure 3-7   **LIBERAL vs. CONSERVATIVE**

Companies and industries can have a wide variance in lending habits and customer requirements. Liberal policies result in a higher number of losses.

| **Liberal** | Higher | RISK | Lower | **Conservative** |

LIBERAL POLICY
Higher losses; little up front credit history investigation; accounts not monitored; terms not strictly enforced.

CONSERVATIVE POLICY
Lower losses; extensive up front credit history investigation; accounts closely monitored; terms strictly enforced.

3.5.1 Credit Screening

Once you have determined that your company must extend credit, set the terms, or the maximum number of days you will allow customers to wait before paying a particular invoice in full. If you establish thirty days for your terms, pretty much a standard for most industries, be prepared to educate your customers about adherence to your conditions. Remember, after thirty days you are likely paying interest to finance your customers and these aged receivables will have no value as collateral against a line of credit. The first phase in the process of managing receivables covers the extension of business credit. Companies that are liberal in their lending habits do very little checking in advance of shipping. They are, of course, at a high risk for loss. Although risk can never be eliminated entirely, it can be reduced substantially by adopting a more conservative approach to credit management. Many companies insist on COD at first and possibly credit card payments. The actual extension of credit terms requires an effective method of screening prospective credit customers and a policy for limiting exposure.

- *Credit Applications:* Credit apps are a key part of the screening process as the application is completed and signed by a principle of the company seeking credit thus agreeing to your organization's terms and conditions. *LIABILITY NOTE:* If the company seeking credit is a sole proprietor or a partnership, the owner(s) are also responsible for the indebtedness. If the applicant is a corporation, the shareholders or directors are not responsible for the debts of the company unless they personally guaranty them. Since most small corporations are private, it will most often be the owner applying for credit. Consider adding a clause on the application whereby the owner guarantees any outstanding amount owed to you from credit purchases they make. There are a number of important pieces of information to include on the application: (*See Figure 3-8.*)

o *Primary Contact Information:* Company name, how long in business, complete mailing and physical address, phone, fax, Email, web site address, and principal(s) name (if the principal(s) are to personally guaranty then obtain their date of birth and possibly social insurance number if permitted in your jurisdiction). Don't be afraid to take down their vehicle plate number as well before they leave your premises.

o *Bank Information:* Include in this section of the application the name of the customer's bank and account number they will be using to write checks for payment of invoices, bank location along with phone number, line of credit and the amount of credit utilized.

o *Trade References:* Have the applicant list at least three trade references that have recently done credit business with them including the supplier's company name, full mailing address, credit contact name, phone, fax, length of time doing business, date of last purchase and credit limit.

• *Credit Reports:* Commercial credit reports are available extensively for North American businesses and at special request globally from *Dun and Bradstreet* and *Equifax*. These reports are available for a fee; an investment that may be well worth the time and expense depending upon your exposure. With one exception, these reports are totally objective and permission is not required to obtain commercial credit information. (Note: In many jurisdictions, consumer credit information cannot be obtained without permission). Commercial credit reports are compiled from legal information (lawsuits and collections) along with payment information from trade suppliers that report customer history. The exception occurs when there is no history and information is compiled through a telephone enquiry. This type of subjective information is collected by some reporting agencies to create a report.

Before purchasing a credit report, ensure that there is a record of payment history, otherwise check for legal items.

- *Credit Groups:* Some commercial credit reporting agencies offer memberships with inclusion in industry credit groups. During monthly meetings, credit professionals meet to discuss accounts. Presenting names of prospective customers to the group may result in timely information that could bring a good customer on board or deny a potentially bad account.

Making the Decision

When you feel that you have collected all of the data available, it is time to make a decision about the applicant's creditworthiness and the amount of credit to extend. But first, there may be some investigation and information verification required on your part.

- *Analyzing Credit Applications:* Credit apps, like resumes, can be very subjective in nature because the person completing them will be biased. Therefore, it is necessary to verify the information before applying any weight to its relevance in making a credit decision.

  o *Contact Information:* Prior to extending large amounts of credit, it may be advisable to visit the prospective customer's facility. This can verify the address, the location where your product may be shipped and the physical state of the company you will be dealing with.

  o *Bank Information:* Don't be afraid to contact the bank as they can verify if the applicant is indeed a customer and for how long. They should also be able to advise you regarding activity levels, any returned items, and possibly the status of any line of credit along with the amount utilized (generally stated by the number of figures).

  o *Trade References:* The weight applied to this criterion is questionable as the applicant is most likely to give you the best suppliers they deal with, possibly a relative. It is still important to contact them by phone or fax a form to the credit department requesting verification of the details submitted on the application.

o *Suspicious Activities:* Be wary of any hesitation on the part of the applicant to answer any questions or give details and be very cautious regarding requests for large one time or first time purchases.

- *Analyzing Credit Reports:* Commercial credit reports (except for those manually produced) are objective in that the information is supplied by unbiased third parties. It is not uncommon to have a disgruntled customer. Therefore, one line of legal information, such as a lawsuit or collection, is not necessarily reason for concern but should be questioned. More than one collection, civil action or a judgment is reason for concern. When analyzing trade information on the report, look for negative trending and recent enquiries. If payment patterns are deteriorating, the applicant may be experiencing financial difficulties, losing suppliers and seeking new sources.

There should be enough information at this point to make an informed decision. The optimal decision would be to extend credit in the amount requested. For this to be the case, the applicant company should have been operating for at least several years with no legal items, a good credit report and a number of satisfied suppliers who are paid on time. If anything negative turns up, either reduce the total amount of credit extended or deny credit altogether leaving them on COD. It may be hard at times to turn down a sale, however, that feeling will quickly disappear if the applicant burns your competitor.

Alternative Methods of Protecting Receivables

There are other methods of protecting receivables so that your company does not have the risk of incurring bad debt. It involves insuring your receivables or selling them to a factoring company. Both alternatives will cost you a commission or a portion of the amount being financed. It is only current receivables that can be financed. There are government agencies that assist, such as the *Economic Development Corporation* (EDC) if you are a Canadian exporter. Two types of factoring are available where receivables are actually purchased. The rate charged for *Factoring with Recourse* is less than that charged in *Factoring without Recourse*. You retain a certain level of liability for unpaid receivables with *Recourse*; otherwise the factoring company assumes the risk.

Figure 3-8   SAMPLE CREDIT APPLICATION

APPLICATION FOR CREDIT

Company Name: _____ Date: _____
Address: _____ City: _____ Zip / Postal: _____
Phone: _____ Fax: _____ Web Site: _____
Years in Business: _____ Type: Sole Proprietor ___ Partnership ___ Corporation ___
Business Description: _____
Bank Name: _____ Account #: _____ Since: _____
Bank Address: _____ City: _____ Zip / Postal: _____
Bank Phone: _____ Line of Credit (Extended / Utilized) $_____ / $ _____
Credit Referrals:
   1. Company Name: _____ Since: _____ Limit: $_____
       Address: _____ City: _____ Zip / Postal: _____
       Phone: _____ Fax: _____ Credit Contact Name: _____
   2. Company Name: _____ Since: _____ Limit: $_____
       Address: _____ City: _____ Zip / Postal: _____
       Phone: _____ Fax: _____ Credit Contact Name: _____
   3. Company Name: _____ Since: _____ Limit: $_____
       Address: _____ City: _____ Zip / Postal: _____
       Phone: _____ Fax: _____ Credit Contact Name: _____
I personally guarantee repayment. Name: _____ Position: _____

Figure 3-8 is a typical credit application illustrating the key information that should be obtained from a new or existing customer asking for credit for the first time. Keep in mind that most small businesses applying for credit will list their best creditors (or friends) as referrals. It is necessary, therefore, to obtain objective information from independent sources such as credit bureaus or your own investigation of the company, depending upon the amount at risk. Simple applications like the one illustrated here can be incorporated in to the company web site as a form and submitted to the credit department for initial screening. Check to ensure the questions you ask are allowed in your jurisdiction.

3.5.2 Monitoring Credit Accounts

Once credit has been extended to a customer and they begin purchasing on terms, it is imperative to make a regular analysis of the aged accounts receivable and their status. There are two methods of monitoring accounts. The primary technique is the *In-House* method which can be combined with the *Commercial Credit Agency Warning* method.

- *In-House:* The *A/R* (*Accounts Receivable*) department prints out the *Aged Receivables* list on a regular basis. *(Every two weeks suggested).* When accounts approach their due date *(within 25 to 28 days on thirty day terms),* make a call. At this point, everyone will answer the phone because they are not in default. It is important that customers honor your terms. Failure to demand adherence to terms gives the customer tacit consent to pay at a later date and take advantage of you. Here is a reality check. If you wait until an account is 45 to 60 days old, chances are better than ninety percent that they will pay at 60 days every time and you are financing them for thirty days. There is also a better than sixty percent chance that the account will go to 90 days plus and an account that reaches 90 days has a thirty percent chance of going to third party action. Most companies will claim that collection reminder calls are made at 45 to 60 days, which implies that customers are allowed 60 days to pay. After 60 days, it is more difficult to reach people for collections. At the 60 day stage of aging, eighty percent of the credit department's time will be spent chasing accounts and only twenty percent collecting money. Making a call as an account is just approaching terms provides the following benefits:

o   80% of your time will be spent collecting accounts and only 20% chasing.

o   The call is friendly, simply asking the customer if the product was received in an undamaged state and reminding them of your thirty day terms. This eliminates any future excuses that the customer did not receive the product or that it was damaged and not acceptable. There is also a customer service flavor added to the call.

o   Ask for another order. This part of the call can substantially increase sales. It may be prudent with new orders to ensure that the promised payment was made before shipping.

•   *Commercial Credit Agency Warning:* Commercial credit reporting agencies such as *Dun & Bradstreet* and *Equifax* offer a valuable account monitoring service to the member companies that provide them with monthly aged receivable information. In addition to the compilation of negative legal data, the collection of payment information makes the credit reports highly objective and very rich in content. In return for the submission of their valuable receivables data, these member companies are generally provided with the following types of warnings:

o   *Legal Items* – a notification if any of their credit customers on the submitted list incurs a legal item including a statement of claim, judgment or a collection action. This allows the subscribing company an opportunity to investigate and take corrective action, such as a credit hold, until the situation is clarified and the risk level improves.

o *Payment Information* – showing how their customers are paying other suppliers. This information is valuable in analyzing payment trending. If the payment habits of a customer begin to show a negative trend, the company may be running into financial difficulty and an investigation may be in order. It will also be apparent if they are paying other suppliers more promptly than you. At this stage a current credit report can be ordered and a re-assessment of the risk conducted. If necessary, a reduction in a customer credit line or a credit hold can be put on an account to prevent a bad debt or further exposure to risk.

o *Credit Groups* – are conducted for certain industries by some commercial agencies in various jurisdictions. Attendance is restricted to credit professionals who share payment and negative information on customers. These meeting are an excellent method for reducing risk.

The monitoring phase of *Receivables Management* is all about awareness. The decision to grant credit has previously been made based upon sound risk assessment, now the task is to deliver this service profitably. This entails eliminating or reducing exposure to bad debt as previously discussed and keeping finance charges low on outstanding receivables. The method for keeping finance charges low is the regular analysis of the *Aged Receivables* report and an understanding of *Days Sales Outstanding (DSO)*.

Days Sales Outstanding (DSO)

Days Sales Outstanding measures the number of times in a year that a company's *Accounts Receivable* turnover. This turnover has a direct relationship with cash flow. The formula to determine *DSO* requires two pieces of information; a determination of your annuals sales and, of course, the total amount in outstanding receivables from your aged receivables report.

Days Sales Outstanding = (Accounts Receivable / Annual Sales) X 365

Example: If annual sales are $1,000,000 and total accounts receivable are $175,000

DSO   =   **(AR / AS) X 365**

(175,000 / 1,000,000) X 365

.175 X 365

DSO   =   **64 days.**

The receivables turn over (365 / 64) = 5.7 times per year. For many industries this would be considered high (DSO of 47 days with a turnover of 7.7 times per year is typically an optimal target). A DSO of 64, in this example company, should be lowered if possible to reduce financing charges and increase cash flow. The aged receivables report for the example above may look similar to the report on the next page.

TOTAL	CURRENT	31 to 60	61 to 90	90+
$175,000.00	107,000.00	52,200.00	12,600.00	3,200.00
100%	61%	30%	7%	2%

The *Aged Receivable* figures listed above are representative of a company that has a relatively liberal approach to credit management. Conservative receivables management would likely prevent aging percentages from reaching these high levels. The 90+ level could represent accounts that may require third party action. The 61 to 90 period should be no higher than 4% (*generally due to special circumstances*), and the 31 to 60 day aging period should be no more than 15% as a target figure. The customers on this report are taking advantage of this organization's generous lending policy, and the company in turn is financing their credit. Reducing the aging percentages to optimal numbers would reduce the outstanding receivables to approximately $138,000. This would in turn reduce the *DSO* to 50 days and the annual turnover would be 7.3 times.

Reducing the *DSO* by 14 days would have a substantial positive effect on cash flow. With annual sales of $1,000,000 - 1 day of sales = $2,740 X 14 = $38,360 increase in cash flow. On a line of credit with a 6% interest rate, the finance charges are $2,300.

These positive results are achieved through customer education in compliance with your terms and collection calls that begin at 25 days instead of the typical 45 days when it is more difficult to collect money. If your customers are currently taking advantage of you, it may take some time to slowly adjust them to your terms; but it can be done with patience, politeness and great customer service.

3.5.3 *Collections*

The best way to look at phase three of receivables management is the scenario of <u>not</u> having to worry about collecting delinquent accounts at all. In a perfect world, all of your customers are a great asset and they all pay on time. Collection activities are costly as it is an indicator that you are financing someone else's debt and you are wasting resources in time and expense to collect it. Good will by this stage has also been exhausted. It is true; a more conservative approach to credit granting will result in lower delinquencies. Unfortunately, even this approach will not totally eliminate them, therefore it is necessary to have a procedure to conduct phase three of the receivables management program. There are a number of steps that a credit collections department will follow. These may vary depending upon the industry standards and specific customer arrangements.

- *Phone Calls:* With thirty day terms, calls should start at 25 to 28 days. (*See Monitoring Accounts*) The second call should be made at 40 days accompanied by a hold on credit if payment is not made within five days. This is a conservative approach and although it may sound harsh, it will cause the customer to adjust to your terms to continue receiving your products and it will prevent further losses. This is most likely to occur with new accounts that have not been properly screened or are testing the waters. If it is an existing account, the important thing is communication as there would have been a business relationship established and there may be a good reason for the delay. Trust is what relationships are built on. If a customer promises payment and doesn't deliver or fails to return calls to discuss their indebtedness, good faith may have been lost. If a customer is honest and open in discussions with suppliers, working with them could result in continued profitable sales with new conditions until their situation improves.

- *Letters:* At sixty days, phone calls result in more chasing than collecting and a demand letter should be considered at seventy-five days if the customer is not responding to collection calls or has broken a promise about making a payment. Some companies use a two or three letter system with the language becoming progressively harsher in tone. I have found, through experience working with one of the larger commercial credit organizations, that the longer it takes to collect, the less likelihood of success. Once an account reaches 120 days past due, the odds of collection using in-house methods, and often third party action, becomes futile. Therefore, a two letter system speeds the process with the first demanding immediate payment within ten days to maintain their account. *(Even if they pay at this point they should go on COD).* If the first letter is not responded to, the second letter will demand payment within ten days or the matter will be handed over to your legal department resulting in a negative occurrence being posted on their credit report.

- *Third Party:* At 120 days turn the account over to a collection agency. (*A more conservative approach would dictate 90 days.*) If the agency collects the account then a commission will be taken from the proceeds. If they cannot collect it, a recommendation is made either to sue or abandon the action.

- *Civil Litigation:* It may be necessary to sue the customer in order to get repayment. If they are being sued by other suppliers, you may want to skip the third party collection action and go straight to litigation to be first in line. This can be a costly venture with a doubtful outcome; therefore, careful consideration must be given to the odds of collecting even if you get a judgment. In large lawsuits, legal costs are very high and most often only the law firms win, especially if the action is defended. Don't throw good money after bad.

Section 4:

operations

4.1 Operational Activities

The third and final module to complete the business plan is *Operations*. Whereas the *Marketing* module is all about the external environment, the processes in the *Financial* and *Operations* modules of an organization are carried out primarily within the internal environment. There are a wide variety of activities encompassed by *Operations* that help an enterprise to function (operate) effectively, efficiently and safely.

- *Facility:* Improvements to office, warehouse or manufacturing space may be required for renters. For some businesses, the purchase of land and buildings, safety equipment and supplies may be required. For owned and leased properties, maintenance – including landscaping or snow removal services – may be needed.

- *Machinery / Equipment:* includes manufacturing machinery leases or purchases along with maintenance and repair; construction or other equipment required to perform services along with regular maintenance and repair; retail operations equipment for inventory control, cash registers, scanners and loss prevention.

- *Warehousing / Logistics:* covers the storage and delivery of product including shipping; procurement, maintenance and repairs to tow motors, reach trucks, and other equipment required to move product in both shipping and receiving; purchase and storage of shipping supplies such as cartons, containers, skids, and shrink wrap; equipment to meet special customer merchandising requirements for packaging and coding SKU numbers.

- *Supply:* includes inventory and the purchase of raw materials for use in manufacturing along with their storage based on production scheduling; packaging materials.

- *Management:* Recruiting experienced candidates for current and future organizational requirements in specialized areas such as finance, marketing, sales, production, operations, IT and human resources.

- *Personnel:* The recruitment, coaching and skills training of qualified employees to fill all required positions in a company.

- *Training / Certification:* Many jurisdictions have strict labor codes requiring a percentage of employees, especially in manufacturing and warehousing, to be certified in first aid. Tow motor, reach truck and heavy equipment operators require appropriate training and certification. The handling of hazardous materials requires special training and certification.

- *I.T.:* All organizations require the processes of *Information Technology*, not only to function efficiently, but also to remain competitive. Technology involves hardware and software; purchasing of up to date desk top / notebook computers, servers, routers, printers, fax machines, copiers, telephone systems; and the appropriate software licensing; and the organization's web site which may also fall into the marketing category if used only for promotion.

It is beyond the scope of this book to go into great detail in all of these operational categories. Many of these areas are specialized and do not have universal business commonality the way that core marketing and business finance concepts are shared. Because of the importance placed on successfully leveraging the Internet, *Creating Effective Business Web Sites* will be covered in this section. Due to the consequence of error for entrepreneurs, sections on *Employee Relations* and *Contingency Planning* are also included.

4.2 Creating Effective Web Sites

There is no denying that the **W**orld **W**ide **W**eb has revolutionized the way we do business and conduct our personal lives. As a business tool, having an effective web site with a solid Internet strategy can give a business a competitive edge – but only if it is done right! There are really only two reasons for a business to have a web presence.

- As a web based business, where your primary method of exchange is through a web site. Web based companies are becoming very popular for new business start-ups. The operating expenses can be substantially lower than a brick and mortar store-front and many functions can be automated allowing them to conduct business 24/7 without human intervention. Unfortunately, it has become very difficult to make money on the Internet. There are millions of other people operating web based businesses. Start-up costs can be high for adequate programming requirements and with the astronomical number of sites competing for visitors, getting the initial message out can be very costly. However, if you do come up with a brilliant idea – something totally unique that no one else is doing – a healthy income can be achieved with the right planning and resources.

- Most businesses will develop a web site as part of their promotional plan. Given the importance of this valuable business tool, it is amazing to see the number of company sites that are outdated in technology or poorly designed. This subject was discussed briefly in the *Marketing* section. However, given the importance of making effective use of web technology in such a competitive environment, the topic is being presented in greater detail here, as part of the *Operations* section. In larger organizations, the company web site is generally maintained by IT department.

There are two ways to utilize resources for the development of a business web site.

- *In-House* methods include doing the development work yourself; having another person in the organization do it, or having a friend / relative create the site. Use caution here that this project is done right, but more on this later.

- *Outsource* to a web developer. There are many good web design and development firms with sound ethics. Unfortunately, this is a totally unregulated industry and there are many who are unqualified and exercise unethical practices. It is definitely wise to outsource this vital aspect of business, but again, use caution and do your homework. This topic is covered later in this chapter with some good advice on choosing the right people to handle your project.

4.2.1 Domains and Intellectual Property

Creating a web presence starts with registering a domain name with an appropriate extension. When typed in the address bar of a web browser, the domain name becomes part of a URL (*Uniform Resource Locator*) or web address along with http:// (*hyper-text transfer protocol*) as a prefix. This is the starting point in the process and the place where many business owners make a number of mistakes. (*See Domain Dos and Don'ts below.*) It is very easy to find and register a domain; the problem here is all of the good names are gone. With millions of domains registered, the United States added new extensions in addition to the popular .com, .net and .org making .biz, .tv and others available for registration. Any person or business can register domain names with one of these common extensions by visiting the web site of a registrar, such as one of the originals, Network Solutions. The process simply involves conducting an on-line search for name availability, registering the domain by submitting a form, then paying by credit card for a specified period of time. There are hundreds of registrars to choose from.

In Canada, domain registrations for the .ca extension are under the control of the Canadian Internet Registration Authority or CIRA. A check for available domain names along with a list of authorized registrars can be found by visiting their site at http://cira.ca and performing a simple search. Each country has a different extension along with specific regulations and restrictions. The United Kingdom requires a double extension showing the type of registration such as .co.uk or .org.uk, whereas most countries simply have the two digit extension, similar to .de for Germany, .ru for Russia or .it for Italy.

When domains are established or renewed with a registrar within a country, the name is then listed with ICANN (*Internet Corporation for Assigned Names and Numbers*), the body which oversees and regulates this process worldwide. The server names (DNS) or location where your domain is to be hosted is also stored by ICANN so that it is available to direct visitors to your web site files. Go to http://icann.org for more information.

Prior to registering an available domain name, you will be required to conduct an on-line search at no charge to see if it is available. The "*Who Is*" search function is available at all registrar sites to determine the ownership status and details of any domain. Search results can indicate that a domain name is available for purchase and registration, but that does not necessarily mean that it can be legally used. Similar to the registration of a business, it is ultimately your responsibility to ensure that there is no infringement on another company's trademark. If there is any doubt, conduct a trademark search as well.

IMPORTANT: On the following page there are a number of suggested Dos and don'ts when it comes to registering domain names. There is one critical detail that should be well noted when completing the registration process. The *Registrant* is the owner of the domain, most often your company name will go here. The *Administrative Contact* is the only person that can make changes to the registration information on file with ICANN at a later date. Some of the important changes you may need to make at any time include the hosting server numbers, address and ownership transfers. The *Administrative Contact Email* is the key ingredient here. No changes are made to any domain name registration details until confirmation is returned to the registrar through this Email. Keep this in mind if you decide to change Email addresses. The *Technical Contact* is of little importance.

Domain Name Dos and Don'ts

- **Do** – choose a name that is short and easy to remember.

- **Do** – register your domain for a minimum of five years. First of all, the rate per year is much lower; and secondly, you won't get annoying renewal notices every year from numerous registrars trying to steal your business.

- **Do** – keep a valid Email address on file for the *Administrative* contact.

- **Do** – keep your domain registration contact information up to date.

- **Do** – keep copies of your registration and renewals in a safe place. A domain name is intellectual property and an asset of your company. In addition to Email verification, most registrar web sites require you to create a profile with a user name and password to manage your domain account. Keep this information in a secure place for future reference. Using a current Email address as your user name can make on-line account management much easier. It can become mind boggling to manage all of the user names and passwords that are assigned to companies doing a high level of business on the Internet. I keep this information in my contact management software. It is attached to the details section of each contact making it very easy to search for a multitude of passwords that can actually be copied and pasted into the browser log-in window.

- **Do** – use your domain name to promote your company. Most businesses will use their web site as part of their promotional plan. Most people will only visit the site if they are sent there by a link or by seeing the web address advertised. Display the domain prominently on vehicles, stationery, marketing collateral, promotional products, and all advertising media. The well designed company web site will provide all of the information that a prospect or customer may require along with a method making it easy to do business with your organization.

- **Don't** – use your company name as a domain name if you expect people to find you through a web search. Search engine ranking is based upon link popularity and the repeated use of key words in the title, meta tags, header text, body text, alternate image text, and more importantly, domain name. When people arrive at your home page, any form of branding and advertising messages that are appropriate to your offering can be displayed regardless of company name.

- **Don't** – let your domain name lapse. On the day that the registration expires, the DNS pointers will no longer direct visitors to your web site. The domain name will appear as being available for registration on a search and someone else can purchase it after thirty days if it is not renewed.

4.2.2 In-House or Outsource?

Each one of these options for developing your company web site has a distinct advantage and disadvantage. Prior to committing resources to the development of this essential business tool, there are some serious considerations. Should the project be tackled *In-House* or *Outsourced* to a web developer.

- ***In-House:*** In the Marketing section, emphasis was put on first impressions and getting one chance to do things right in such a competitive environment. *Image is everything* in developing a web site as well. So why do so many small business owners cut corners in such a key area of business operations? A common method for saving money at the expense of launching a good web presence is having a friend or relative (*who knows a little about FrontPage*) develop the site. There are many programs that will create web pages, however, the code they create can be quite messy and formatting is not always provided to support all browser types. Although, most people use *MS Internet Explorer*, the *Mozilla Firefox* browser is becoming quite popular and *Google Chrome* is earning a following. If there are budget restraints, it would be practical to outsource the project in phases rather than taking a chance on developing a complete web site that either doesn't work properly or conveys a questionable image. If any of the following conditions cannot be satisfied, serious consideration should be given to outsourcing the task to a professional web developer.

  o *Expertise* is necessary to produce a product that will meet current W3C (*World Wide Web Consortium*) standards. This is a must to provide accessibility to a majority of visitors for proper viewing and search engine bots for accurate page indexing. This also means that the person developing the site should be able to write, at a minimum, basic html so that inappropriate code can be identified, corrected and appropriate code inserted to meet standard. An understanding of CSS, JavaScript, Flash, php scripting and databases may be required to create necessary functionality. There are also important standards that must be met for good web site design. These are described later in this chapter.

  o Professional Tools are a must to create an effective and functional product. *Web Development* refers more to code and structure where software products such as Adobe *Dreamweaver* and *Flash* are common programs. *Web Design* refers more to the look and content of a web site with Adobe *Illustrator and Photoshop* on top of the preferred list by top designers. There are other professional programs available and code can actually be written in a simple text editing program like *Notepad*. However, the absence of appropriate software makes the optimization of photos, the creation of appropriate graphics and high quality portable documents (pdf's) impossible. Since Adobe purchased Macromedia, some great all in one packages are now available incorporating the best of development and design tools. My office utilizes the *Adobe Creative Suite Web Premium* package which combines *Dreamweaver*, *Flash*, *Photoshop*, *Illustrator* and *Acrobat* along with other programs at a cost that is much lower than purchasing the programs individually. Check the Adobe web site or conduct a web search for *web authoring programs*. There are some great free web developer tools and training aids available on-line.

o   *Development Time* can be substantial and unless you have a dedicated person on staff in a technical capacity, it may be better to outsource. Should you decide to tackle this project yourself, keep in mind the areas of business where your talents may be more effectively utilized. A small business owner's ability to generate sales will often far outweigh the cost of outsourcing to a professional web developer.

• *The Best of Both* is another option open to business owners. Outsource the development and design to a professional and have them structure the pages so that you or a staff member can make changes to text and graphics when required. Programs like Adobe's *Contribute* have an easy to use browser interface with *WYSIWYG (What You See Is What You Get)* functionality. This makes it easy to keep content fresh and save the company on maintenance fees down the road. You will use the ftp address, user name and password to access to the server for changes to be published.

• ***Outsource:*** Most small businesses will need to outsource their web project in order to launch a site that is both functional and has an image worthy of your branding. Due to the fact that this industry is unregulated, it is important to use caution here and do your homework before assigning this important task to a stranger. Although there are many reputable and ethical web design and development firms, there are unfortunately, many more that are unqualified or unscrupulous. I have personally assisted many small business owners who have been victimized by unethical web development practices. The following suggestions should help to ensure that you are choosing an outsource partner that will provide solutions and not nightmares.

o *References* from satisfied customers and a portfolio of completed work are the best indicators of credibility. Look at sites the web developer has created and contact the business owner. Ask if they are pleased with the site and the results they are getting from it. Also find out if the developer stayed within the quoted prices and delivered within the promised time frame. Finally, look at the bottom of each home page on the listed web sites to see if there is a *Copyright* notice.

o *Copyright* is another process of protecting intellectual property. There are certain types of work that are automatically protected by copyright when created. These include literary works such as books or articles, photographs, music, screen plays and web sites. Any piece of work that is protected by copyright cannot be copied or used without the owner's permission. The key word here is *owner*. In the previous clause it was suggested to look at the bottom of sample web site home pages for a copyright notice. If the web developer or designer lists their own name as owner of the copyright, go somewhere else. This is a highly unethical and common practice that can lead to nightmares for the unsuspecting company that hired them in good faith believing that they owned their own web site. If the web developer's name appears here, then they own the code and technically, you cannot make changes without their authorization. Should you have a falling out, they may not let you have your site files to take with you if a transfer to another server is your intention. You may have to start from scratch. This is a very underhanded way to handcuff a customer and it happens all the time. Whatever happened to retaining customers through quality work and great service? The bottom line here: you are paying for it and you should own it!

o *Domain Registrations* conducted on your behalf by web developers can also result in a similar nightmarish scenario where they put their company name as *Domain Owner* and / or their own name as *Administrative Contact*. In the first example, if you have a falling out, as the registered owner, they can keep the domain and you must try to find a new one. This could be a potentially costly and embarrassing situation to be in if you have a substantial customer base doing business with you over the web. In the second example of unscrupulous behavior, no transfers of ownership or changes in named servers can be initiated without the developer's consent – and they must make the request! Make certain that you handle your own domain registrations so you have control and list yourself as the *Administrative Contact*. Changes to registration information are made by logging in to your account on the domain registrar's web site so keep the user name and password in a safe place.

o *Contracts* are a necessary part of doing safe business, especially with trades or outsourced contractors. There are many very good web developer / designers out there. When you find one after doing your homework, insist on a contract. This protects both parties and makes the web developer accountable to perform while you, the customer, are accountable to pay if they fulfill their obligation. The contract should specify the total cost; details of work to be performed; and a date for completion. Be sure they include the following clauses: that you or your company owns the copyright; the web developer will deliver to you, the customer, all completed web folders and original files used to develop the final site; and include a confidentiality clause if they will have access to sensitive customer or business information. Having control of your domain, ownership of the code or site copyright, and all original files, allows you to go wherever you want and whenever you want.

o *A Web Development Plan* is a must if your web site is going to work for your company and have any chance of producing a return on investment. It will also help to reduce development costs. You can expect to pay upwards from two thousand dollars for a basic site to five thousand dollars and up for a more complex design. Graphic production, artwork preparation, Flash animation, databases, and special programming will add to this amount. If you cannot afford to develop the entire project right away, web sites can be developed in stages so complete one phase at a time as you can afford to do it.

4.2.3 The Web Development Plan

In order to design a strategy, a plan must be developed. It could be a business plan; marketing plan; media plan; sales plan; contingency plan; recruiting plan; or any plan needed to fit the scope of the desired objectives. So why not create a web development plan? The reason why most business owners say their web site doesn't produce results is generally due to the fact that there was no plan created during the initial stages of design and development. A web developer or other person typically would be contacted and handed a brochure along with instructions just to create a site. It is often up to the designer or developer to come up with some kind of look utilizing the company logo and color scheme. There is a better way – developing a sound plan then moving forward with an Internet strategy that has a great chance of providing results. There are many benefits that can be anticipated from a properly developed web site, however there are also limitations. Understanding these limitations will help in creating a plan with achievable objectives.

As alluded to earlier in this section, a company web site is almost always an extension of the promotional plan. The exception occurs when a company operates a web business where all transactions take place over the Internet. In this case, all business planning and strategy development centers around the Internet plan which would be heavily weighted in IT management, programming and the functionality of taking orders, accepting payment then ensuring speedy order fulfillment in an automated environment. Operating this type of business is a subject that is beyond the scope of this publication. This section will concentrate on web development for the conventional brick and mortar small business. If you decide that your business is to be web based, most of the principles outlined in this book still apply. Some of the more popular web based businesses are directories or industry specific applications. Many people today are developing web businesses and their revenue model is based entirely on Google Ad Sense. (*You receive revenue when visitors click on the ads posted on your site*). This is a low cost business venture which only works if you can generate a substantial amount of traffic to generate the impressions and click-through visitation. As is the case with most other web business ideas, there is a tremendous amount of competition and without spending a large sum on promotion, a totally unique idea or niche is required for your key words to score high. Much information is available on-line from Google Ad Sense to learn about the subject. Keep one thing in mind – there is really no quick and easy was to earn a fortune on the Internet. Almost every great idea has been tried. Or has it? You be the judge and do your homework.

Companies Operating Locally or Regionally

When small business owners are asked about their own expectations from the web site, most will put sales at the top of the list anticipating that prospective customers will find them over the Internet. In reality, unless your business sells globally or nationally, don't waste your time and resources expecting people to find you by typing key words in a search engine. A business that operates in a narrow geographic area, will receive most visitors to their site because they were directed there through some form of advertising or signage. Consumers are still more likely to use a directory (*including local web directories*) or the yellow pages to locate a local trade or retail business. Your web site design should still be search engine friendly as there will always be some visitors who find your site through searches, however, the strategy should not be built around this expectation.

Companies Operating Nationally or Globally

It is called the *World Wide Web* for a reason, and if you are selling nationally or globally it would be worthwhile to design part of your strategy around developing high search engine rankings. Keep in mind that there could be thousands of other sites competing for the same visitor pool and the more common your key words, the harder it is to get on the first page of results without paying to be there. All web sites will eventually be located and indexed by major search engines and start receiving visitors from many different countries worldwide. Your company can only take advantage of this traffic if the scope of your sales has a broader base.

Determining a Fit for Functionality

There are many things that a well designed and developed web site can do for an organization. Depending on your business type and industry, any of these areas may be considered to provide greater functionality and add to your return on investment. A *B2B* will lean heavily on sales tools, simplicity of ordering, customer service and technical support as most of the visitors to the web site will see it for the first time when they are a customer. A typical *B2C* may rely more on product information, location maps, rates sheets, hours of business and contests. The main purpose here would be to convert visitors who found the site through advertising, into customers. Here are some areas of functionality that can be built in to a company site. Determine which processes can be expected to bring results to a business like yours then design the functionality in to your plan.

Product / Service Information: The company web site is <u>the</u> forum to showcase your products and services. Many products can be listed on a single page with a brief description, thumb nail photo, and link to another page featuring a larger photo and more detail. The web has also made it possible to deliver product or service specifications on high quality pdf (*Portable Document Format*) files developed by Adobe that can be downloaded instantly and printed in color by the recipient virtually eliminating printing and distribution costs.

Log In: Customers or members can have their own password protected area of the web site. A convenient log-in box on the home page can open a dynamic page that is personalized for the customer giving them access to areas no other visitor can use such as secure ordering and technical or customer service support. The use of mysql databases and php code has made increased functionality in sites very affordable.

Photo Tour: Retailers or any other type of business with a customer showroom can set up a high quality photo tour and floor plan right on their web site. Flash is a perfect tool for integrating photos or video clips with user controls.

Placing Orders: Processes to take orders can vary in complexity from complete systems that fulfill, restock and invoice automatically to simple form submissions delivered to a staff member who looks after the order details.

Accepting Payment: Integrating merchant account services such as *Pay Pal* in to the site can offer your customers the convenience of paying securely on-line by debit or credit card. The fees are reasonable compared with other merchant account providers and the setup is easy.

Tracking Shipments: Major couriers and the commercial division of the postal service can provide software and a web interface that will allow customers to track their own shipments.

Credit Applications: Businesses that offer customer credit accounts can accept applications that are submitted through simple forms right on the company web site. The form can collect all of the information necessary to make a decision.

Upon submission an Email would be generated and sent to the credit department for processing.

Company Contacts: The company address, phone / fax numbers and important Email addresses make it easy for customers to get service or technical support through specially posted links or forms on the page.

Employment Opportunities: More and more employees are finding work by checking company web sites. It is important to have links from local job and employment centers in order to get the traffic. Optimizing the employment page with the right keywords can also work to gain high search engine ranking in a local area to attract these targeted visitors. Specific terms such as: *"upper new york state employment opportunities"* or *"southern ontario employment"* will get higher ranking than *"ontario employment"* or *"new york jobs"* because of the number of sites competing for those key words.

Press Room: Press Releases and other events can be posted on your own special page with abridged articles and photos. Complete articles for download in pdf format can be made available through links on the page.

Testimonials: References from satisfied customers dispel doubt and skepticism.

Brochures and Sales Tools: The company web site has become an invaluable resource for the sales force providing instant access to high quality pdf brochures and product specification sheets. A prospect or customer can click on the company web site and be guided by a sales rep to the appropriate information. Download functionality provides instant access and quicker sales versus the expense and time delay of mailing a package the conventional way then following up.

Technical Support: Technical support and customer service consume a high level of company resources in staff hours. Providing all of the most common information right on the company web site can boost customer satisfaction and provide a high return on investment in the reallocation of valuable resources. Some of the most popular support areas include: posting an FAQ page that answers all of the most frequently asked questions; making owner and service manuals available for download in pdf format; setting up a searchable knowledge base to answer technical support questions; posting a bulletin board or forum in a password protected customer area of the site where they can post questions and discuss your products with others. There are free *open source* bulletin board applications available on the web that work very well.

Location Maps: Quality maps are available free from many sources on the Internet to post on your web site and guide visitors to your location including interactive maps from Google and other sources.

Email Marketing: Special offers can be posted on *customer only* pages on the site that can be accessed by a link provided in customer Email messages.

Contests: Posting a contest application form on your site is a great way to collect new contact information for your sales database along with valuable marketing information collected from questions that are answered prior to form submission.

Surveys: Customer retention requires the collection of important information regarding your performance as a supplier and the most convenient way to accomplish this is through a form posted on the company web site.

Intranet: A corporate web site can also be created that is hosted internally on your own network (LAN or WAN) servers and not available outside the company firewall. This set up, known as an *Intranet* site, is ideal for posting employee resources, training material and internal company bulletins.

The Flow Chart

Once you have determined what web site functionality will work for your company, it is time to lay out the project and the best way to do that is with a flow chart. The work flow is laid out to assist the web developer in designing the site to give you the functionality and navigation required. This will take the guess work out of the site assembly and save you considerable development costs. There are a number of ways to create flow charts and the preference is yours, however, the method described here is very simple and easy to follow. The set up is similar to a site map on a web site with an expandable tree exposing the tiers of web pages. The Home page is the tier one page with hyperlinks to tier two pages. These pages may have links to tier three and there are occasions when a tier four page is necessary. Another way to reduce development costs is to do some research on-line and pick out a few web sites that you like. Give the list of site addresses to your web designer and it will be clear about the type of navigation system, color scheme and layout designs that will work for you. It is infringing on a copyright to duplicate another company's design, however, using ideas from various areas and sites can create something new that is unique for your company. Instead of the web designer guessing and coming back to you with numerous costly revisions, an acceptable final layout can be developed in less time and with less expense.

Hosting and Maintenance

When your new company site is completed, it must be hosted on a web server for the world to see. There are two alternatives: host on your own server or purchase a plan from a company that specializes in web hosting. Most small businesses do not have the in-house resources to host their own site. It requires a high speed, high bandwidth dedicated connection to the Internet and the server must be running twenty-four hours per day. There must also be back up power capabilities and technical support available to recover the operating system from crashes. Software must also be upgraded when newer versions are released. Signing up with a hosting company is the best bet for most small businesses and a web search will return thousands of names.

Many web developers provide a hosting service, often as a reseller. They may be able to provide you with a service package that includes periodic maintenance and web changes along with hosting. As your business show piece is being constructed, the developer should be able to provide a link allowing you to see the progress. Prior to launch date, a choice must be made regarding the hosting service. A number of important questions must be answered to protect your investment and keep the site running worry free. When the choice is made, the server names must be assigned or changed through your domain registrar by the *Administrative Contact*. The web folders and files will be uploaded to the server and when the pointers are in place at ICANN you can start measuring the traffic. Consider the following when choosing a web hosting service:

- *Location* of the servers is not an issue, after all it is the World Wide Web and any location on the globe is just a click and a few seconds away. The location of the servers in relation to the Internet trunk may be an issue for a high traffic site from a bandwidth perspective. Learn these facts from the hosting company and ask how long they have been in business.

- *Prices* vary considerably from one company to another and added services such as secure servers and databases may increase the cost. Basic hosting is not expensive and free hosting is available with a catch – you will see someone else's ads all over your site.

- *Statistics* are critical to measuring the performance of your web site. Statistics server software has become very sophisticated so be sure that your hosting company can provide you with access to these important customizable reports. Retrieve your web site stats at least monthly to learn how many unique visitors came to your site. *(The term hits is quite common, unfortunately it is meaningless in measuring traffic. A hit occurs every time a file is called off the server through the code being read by the browser. A page can have dozens of files such as images including each instance of a navigation button, therefore the same number of hits. Unique IP addresses are a more meaningful measure of traffic, as are page views or impressions.)* Other key monthly statistics include: pages viewed the most; entry pages (*it is not only your home or index page that will appear in search results – other pages can be optimized as well*); referrals to see which sites are sending traffic; media downloads such as pdf brochures; and key phrases used to find your web site in search engines. The geographic origin of the visitor is also available along with common browser types and operating systems.

- *Support* along with data storage and recovery are worth enquiring about with a prospective hosting company. These issues are very important as servers can develop problems that must be dealt with quickly to stay on-line. Keep in mind that support is for server issues only. It doesn't cover web site problems that are regular development or maintenance issues, such as forms that do not work properly.

- *Server Software* should be current to maintain full functionality. This includes the latest releases of mysql, phpmyadmin, and other common applications that should be supported if your future development needs require them.

- *Domain Based Email* addresses are important to you and your staff for branding purposes. It is much more professional for a customer to send an Email to a business address, such as jthompson@yourcompany.com rather than jt_thunderchicken@hotmail.com. Your business Email address, info@yourbusiness.net should appear on the web site near your phone number. Several business Email addresses can be set up on the site for sales, service, info, reservations, etc. and one or all can be forwarded seamlessly to your personal Email providing the type of professional branding visitors should see. If you find that the posted addresses are subjected to spam, consider a link to a web form that is forwarded to the appropriate address. Forms can be spam protected by the inclusion of *captcha* image verification and form field validation.

4.2.4 Web Development Dos and Don'ts

- *Do* - use current *W3C (World Wide Web Consortium)* code standards for accessibility and functionality. Some search engines base returns on proper code as one of their ranking criteria.

- *Do* - make your web site user friendly. You have thousands of competitors and if a visitor gets frustrated looking for something they will leave and never return. This means providing a great navigation system for visitors to find what they are looking for quickly and easily within the site. In addition to having a consistent look and feel, each page should have a standard set of navigation buttons and it should always be clear to the visitor which page they are viewing. Consider adding a *Site Map* or search function. In addition to graphic navigation buttons, add text links to the page footers. Search engine bots that visit your site like to follow text links to index all pages of your site for inclusion in search results. Use the *alt tag* on photos so that those with accessibility issues and visitors who turn off images in their browser can view appropriate data in lieu of photos.

- *Do* - brand yourself using outstanding graphics, design and complimentary colors. Remember the line *Image is Everything* and that you get one chance to make a good first impression. Photos are great but keep them small and crisp to avoid distracting from the message or the visitor's ability to easily find the information they are looking for. Carry the same look throughout the site with your company logo, name and tag line on a small header graphic. Save most of the room on the home page for rich content.

- *Do* - change *Home* page content often to keep it rich, current and brief. Search engine spiders are always looking for fresh content and they reward in ranking.

- ***Do*** - put your own copyright © notice on the bottom of the *Home* page.

- ***Do*** - optimize your web site for search engines. Even if you will be directing most visitors to the site, a properly optimized page will get a higher search engine ranking and some targeted traffic. To accomplish this determine the key words someone would use to find your business. These words must be included in the *title* – this is the text that appears on the header bar of the browser and the title line on search results. Include these words in the Meta tags, both *keyword* and *description*, as this is the phrase that appears on search results. The same words must be repeated in the *header* text, *body* text and photo *alt* tags on the page.

- ***Do*** - keep the file sizes small on the *Home* page. There are still people in remote areas using dial up connections and if the page takes too long to load they will go somewhere else. Photographs are the worst offenders here so keep the file size small.

- ***Don't*** - create a home page that scrolls forever. Keep the arrival page to no more than two screen views. A major problem in many web sites is a desire to cram everything the company offers on the first page. (*Does this sound familiar as one of the top ten marketing mistakes?*) The visitor is likely looking for one area of interest and if they are forced to read through everything else you do, they will quickly become frustrated and go somewhere else. Make the design simple and clean with a brief and concise key description on each product or service area. The visitor can quickly locate the information important to their needs and click the link to a page with more specific details.

- ***Don't*** - use sound on your site and force people to search for their mute control. Sounds can be very distracting and not everyone has your taste. There is a place for sound files on some web sites, however, to be utilized properly the visitor must be allowed to activate the control – if they want to.

- ***Don't*** - use splash pages. These are pages that are often created totally in *Flash* and force a visitor to wait or click *Skip Intro* to find the good stuff. By then many have gone somewhere else. Visitors are valuable and to lose them for the sake of having a pretty animated entry page does not make good sense. Splash or intro pages are also not search engine friendly.

- ***Don't*** - use frames or create sites totally in *Flash* if you expect people to find you through searches. These designs are <u>not</u> search engine friendly and *Flash* sites can take forever to load if they are not developed to stream properly. Flash is a powerful tool capable of producing high impact results with added functionality, but only if used properly.

Promoting Your Site

Most visitors to a corporate web site are directed there through advertising. Print your web address on everything that goes out of the office including stationery, business cards, signage, promotional products, advertising, vehicles, and Emails. All Email should use the company domain based address and the body should have the appropriate signature file on the template. This file includes your name, company name, tag line, address, phone and a link to the web site. Keep in mind, that by directing someone to your web site, all company product / service and contact information is at their fingertips.

If you want visitors to find your site through web searches, the pages must be optimized to be search engine friendly as previously described. Repeating key words is only part of the engine algorithm. Ranking is becoming more weighted to link popularity and key words in the body text making results more relevant. Find high quality sites that will exchange links but make sure they are a resource for your business and visitors. As part of your media plan, it may be necessary to purchase links on high traffic sites that your target audience may visit. Submit your site to search engines. It is also possible to purchase higher ranking. An account with *Google Ad Words* is cost effective and allows you to set your own key word *pay per click* budget with a credit card deposit. Every time a visitor clicks on your listing there is a small withdrawal from your account. *Yahoo Search Marketing* is a similar resource where you bid on each keyword.

Leveraging Social Media

Another popular method of promoting your web site is through the use of social networking web sites. Some of the most popular sites in relation to web site promotion are *Facebook, Twitter, LinkedIn,* and *Google* sites such as *You Tube.* The great thing about this method of promotion is that there is no charge.

- <u>*Facebook*</u>: There are two faces to *Facebook*, personal and business. Open a business account that is separate from your personal account and build your free site with photos, descriptions, contact information and a link to your site. Be sure to put a link to your Facebook page on your web site.

- *Twitter*: There are two reasons for a business to be on *Twitter*: to share information about your organization by *tweeting;* or learning about customers and the competition as a listener. Open your business account and decide how you will utilize the resource. If you want to learn about other companies, conduct a search of their name. More information about using *Twitter* for business is available on the site.

- *LinkedIn*: This is a professional networking site where you can post your free business and personal profile. *LinkedIn* provides pure networking opportunities and methods to source out resources for your business. Visit the *LinkedIn* Learning Center for more information.

- *Google*: It is possible to open a single *Google* account to encompass all of your activities with these powerful web resources including Google's *Ad Words, Ad Sense, Analytics, Places, Webmaster Tools,* and *YouTube.* You can access the login page to each of these resources using their own unique url yet, for the sake of simplicity, access each with a single user name and password. For security reasons, change your password frequently.

  o *YouTube:* On *YouTube,* develop some quality video clips and upload them with a description and link to your own web site. You can also add the code to your site which embeds the video directly from the *YouTube servers.*

  o *Google Places:* Allows you to post your business information with photos, description, contact numbers and url directly on the *Google* Maps return page showing your location on the map.

  o *Google Webmaster Tools / Analytics:* These free services allow you to receive valuable information about your site's performance.

Measuring Web Results

As with tracking media results to ascertain how your customers find out about your product or services, it is also very important to track the results from your web planning to confirm things you are doing right and identify things that can be improved. There are several ways to do this.

- *Web Server Statistics*: As mentioned previously in this chapter, your hosting service should provide you with access to web server statistics providing valuable visitor information such as: unique visits; most viewed pages; entry pages; downloads; referring web sites; search terms; and geographic source of traffic to name a few. These reports can often be customized and automated to be sent to you as regular Email messages.

- *Google Analytics*: This is a free tracking service that measures web site traffic. Combined with *Ad Words*, valuable marketing results are returned on your key word campaigns. After setting up your *Analytics* account, a snippet of code is provided to paste on the page to be tracked.

- *Search Engine Reporting*: Programs, such as *Web Position*, allow you to run regular reports showing the rank of each search term in selected search engines. It also shows if terms are trending upward or losing ground.

4.3 Employee Relations

As your small business grows, employees will become your most valuable asset. They are expected to deliver skill, productivity and reliability in return for a fair compensation and a healthy working environment. Employees, in any capacity, are also the biggest ambassadors of your product or service and the individuals that can make the biggest impact on customers. There are many aspects of employee relations that must be understood and subscribed to by small business owners. The following is a list of some of the more obvious areas that can have a major impact on your operation. These are divided into two separate time frames. The first is a list of important considerations when recruiting an employee and the second details important factors to consider for retaining and motivating the people you have hired.

4.3.1 Planning and Recruiting

The best way to avoid problems with employees after they are hired is to do a good job at the planning and recruiting level. Although there is a probationary period in your favor, usually three months, the expense of recruiting and training during that time along with lost productivity provide great incentives for doing it right from the start. Growth in any small business must be well planned to provide sustainable profitability. The two most common types of growth in a small business are facility along with production equipment and the addition of new employees, both of which must be carefully planned as there is a substantial cost to each – fixed cost. Part of a business plan is the *Operations* section which outlines how the company will establish, maintain and expand all of the operational processes and components that were listed earlier. This includes drafting a plan to accommodate new employees and management personnel. The best way to do this is to look ahead at your business in one year, two years, three years and five years. As sales grow, the need for new employees to fill important positions may be substantiated.

A new employee comes with a price tag, not only a wage or salary, but benefits such as: employment insurance, employer's share of government pension, and expenses related directly to payroll such as Worker's Compensation coverage and medical benefits if applicable. All of these costs must be considered at each stage of development as they are a fixed cost that must be met every month regardless of sales. A small business owner may find it necessary to add an employee to take orders and do clerical work when it is realized that they cannot keep wearing a large number of hats. A new employee can free up a great deal of time for the business owner, who in turn can more than offset the additional cost with increased sales. The small business owner may find it necessary to hire a new salesperson. It is relatively straight forward to calculate the performance in sales volume required from the new rep based on knowing your margins. This also helps in the assignment of objectives and bonus levels.

In establishing a growth plan for human resources, an easy way to lay out objectives and requirements is to draft an *Organizational Chart (Org Chart – see Figure 4-1)* for each year. The timing for the addition of new employees and the department where a vacancy must be filled can be established by looking at the sales growth figures on the *Profit and Loss* projections. For each projected year, create a simple organizational chart showing where new positions must be filled. Some *Microsoft Office* programs have *SmartArt* functionality to create these charts.

Figure 4-1 **SAMPLE ORG CHARTS** *for a small distribution company.*

Year Two

Basic company set up with one individual handling all warehousing tasks including receiving, order fulfillment and shipping. Another full-time employee is responsible for all clerical duties including bookkeeping, collections and customer service. The owner manages all key business areas *(Finance, Marketing, and Operations)* with the majority of time being devoted to selling and purchasing.

Year Three

The owner is strained to find the time required for sales and the growth potential is such that the addition of a salesperson is more than justified. The owner continues to manage all key business areas.

Year Five

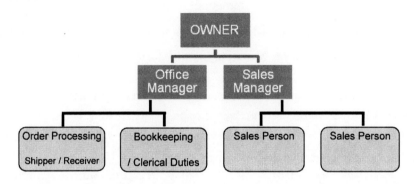

The owner is not able to manage all areas of the business from a time perspective and growth has substantiated the addition of two key members of the management team. All clerical and warehousing personnel now report directly to the *Office Manager* while all sales personnel report directly to the *Sales Manager*. New employees would report directly to the appropriate manager who in turn reports directly to the owner. The owner has the time to concentrate on key areas of a growing company such as banking relations, financial management, marketing, facility, IT *(outsourced)*, employee relations and purchasing. Finance, *IT* and *Human Resources* specialists would be added as the company grows further and expertise in these departments is required.

Job Descriptions

In planning for new employees, the creation of a detailed job description for each position is imperative for a number of reasons. A concise job description leaves no doubt in an employee's mind as to the company's expectations of them. The description will also form the basis of your recruitment ads and interview criteria. The following should be included in a job description:

Job Title.

- Complete description of all duties that the company will expect the person to perform.

- Education, certification, experience and skill requirements for the position.

- Location of the employee's work place. (Company office or facility, home office, travel, etc.)

- Hours of work.

- Driving and license requirements.

- Salary or wage range for entry level in the position may be included.

- Area on the form for Name, Signature, Date and Witness Signature.

The job description should be one of several important documents the new employee signs and receives a copy of when they accept your offer of employment. Aside from government taxation forms, other documents to consider in collaboration with your company lawyer are *Confidentiality* and *Non Competition* agreements. These are to protect the company interests if the employee leaves. Breach of the confidentially agreement is generally very difficult to prove. It is extremely hard to safeguard critical customer information, however, non competition agreements are standard for two years and certain employees are expected to honor these or face litigation. This agreement does not prevent the employee from working in the same industry – just starting up a company within a certain time frame to compete directly against you. Also consider drafting a *Code of Conduct* requiring respect of fellow employees, prevention of harassment, and use of company Internet and technology.

Employee Related Legislation

It is the responsibility of company management to be aware of and abide by all employee related legislation and workplace requirements. The following areas are applicable to most business:

- Human Rights legislation at all levels of government.

- Employment standards related to hours of work, minimum wage, vacation pay, probationary periods and employee termination.

- Employee Health and Safety – providing the necessary equipment and assuring a safe and healthy workplace environment.

- Worker's Compensation or any applicable benefit to compensate employees who are injured on the job – premiums are the employer's responsibility.

- Training and Licensing for specialized positions and equipment operation ensure a high level of competency and reduce senseless accidents that prevent an employee from going home to their family.

It is the employer's responsibility to ensure that employees in certain positions, such as heavy equipment operators, are trained and properly certified.

- First Aid trained employees and medical supplies must be available to assist any employee injured while awaiting the arrival of emergency personnel.

- Planning must be clear to all employees on *Steps to Follow* in case of an emergency such as a serious injury, fire or severe weather.

Failure to look after employee safety can result in severe penalties.

Finding the Right Person

Good people are hard to find and when they are recruited, it is in your best interest to provide an environment that will encourage them to stay. The best way to accomplish this is to hire wisely with a set of criteria that help to ensure that the person is a good fit for the company – *and* that the company is a good fit for the person. Candidates for a position can be located by registering with government sponsored placement centers, placing ads in newspapers, the company web site employment opportunities page and word of mouth or referrals from trusted sources.

Request a resume from the individuals for pre-screening purposes advising that only those selected for interviews will be contacted. This will allow you to sort the submissions into three piles: ones that are automatically rejected because they clearly do not meet your requirements as detailed on the job description; an "A" stack for those applicants who will definitely receive a call; and the balance in the "B" folder that will be kept on file or referred to if a selection cannot be made from the "A" pile. It is courteous and professional to send a letter to those not being invited for an interview thanking them for considering your company and advising that you will hold their resume on file.

A phone call to the "A" candidates can validate some of the resume material regarding employment and skills. This personal contact will also give you a feel for the *fit* and a decision can be made whether to invite them for a personal interview. Advise the candidate what they should expect at the interview and what to bring with them such as a copy of reference letters, certificates of achievement, and company awards from employers. It is important to keep in mind that the individual may be currently employed and you should not contact their employer without their permission. This does not usually happen until an offer is at hand, however, previous employers can be contacted, and again it is advisable to solicit your candidate's permission before calling. Some important considerations during this phase of recruiting include:

- *Politically Correct Questions* – know the right questions to ask and be aware of the wrong questions that can actually get you in trouble. There are some very good books available that cover the topic of questions to ask during an interview.

- *Resumes* – are a good screening tool only. Many people will not only exaggerate on a resume, but also commit to outright lies about education, experience, and skills just to get the job. Some people are also experts at the interview process.

- *Role Play* – is the best way to confirm skills. If computer skills are necessary for the position, have the candidate prepare a spreadsheet or other document. For sales positions, the candidate should be able to sell you something, or even your own product or service. This is a good way to create a short list.

- *Knowledge* – about your company and industry shows that the person has done their homework and has an interest. The candidate's questions should also be about a fit. Learn about their career expectations over the next five to ten years.

- *Validate* – all supplied information once you have created a short list and receive the candidate's permission to contact employers. When contacting a previous employer, the name of someone who is going to give a shining report will likely appear on the list. Ask that person for the name of another supervisor and speak with them to get an objective opinion. Bonding companies can look after the candidate's background checks if this process is required for certain positions.

4.3.2 Coaching and Compensating

Employee or Contractor?

First of all, a word of caution regarding a practice that appears to be happening more frequently, especially with small businesses. It is not uncommon for small companies to take on a new employee under the condition that they act as a contractor, responsible for paying their own taxes and providing their own benefits. In this way, the company feels that they can avoid collecting income taxes, paying their share of government pensions, providing liability insurance including payments for worker's compensation premiums, and other legitimate employee deductions. This does work at times, but beware if an employee suffers an injury at work or complains to labor authorities. The federal government does not have a sense of humor when companies cut corners in the area of human resources to save money.

Under some circumstances a person may be considered a contractor, however if certain criteria are not met when scrutinized, a small business could find themselves in hot water with requirements to pay substantial fines, back taxes and employee benefits. Some of these criteria include:

- *Tools* – if the worker uses their own tools to carry out the job, the indication is that they may be a contractor.

- *Location* – if a worker goes to the same place to perform their job every day, there is a greater likelihood that they should be classified as an employee.

- *Single Employer* – should an individual perform duties for more than one company in the course of a typical week or month, there is a case that they could be treated as a contractor.

Employee Handbook

Once a new employee comes on board, it is the responsibility of the employer to provide them with the training and tools necessary to be successful and reach their full potential in their position. Of course, this benefits both parties as satisfied employees provide value and productivity for the employer. One way to make an employee's life at work much easier is to take the guess work out of company expectations. This can be accomplished by writing a job description as described earlier, and developing an employee handbook. This book will list the policy of the company as it relates to every aspect of employee behavior or actions that can have a detrimental effect on the work environment for others or cause problems for smooth company operations and profitability. This really is a *catch all* line and more specifics need to be written, such as adhering to basic human rights in all dealings with other people; theft from the company; an Email policy to prevent incoming viruses from friends infiltrating and shutting down the company computer network; surfing the Internet for pleasure on company time; excessive absenteeism; and insubordination to name a few. The possible consequences should also be listed and some will include immediate termination. There is no question left in the employee's mind as to the immediate remedy for certain actions.

The book should also include some of the benefits the employee is entitled to, even if there are no formal supplemental medical benefits provided. These may include bereavement leave for a death in the family specifying the length of time; vacation entitlement incremental to a specified number of years service; sick time entitlement; training or extended learning allowances; and any other applicable benefits offered.

Employee Retention

There are a number of reasons why small business owners can be very difficult to work for, and most don't realize it. Since employees are such an important part of business branding and profitability, and good people are hard to find, it logically follows that there must be some kind of retention strategy in place. Productive and reliable employees are worth their weight in gold to a business. High employee turnover is costly in recruiting time, training and learning curve, along with lost productivity. The following lists some of the mistakes made by small business owners and possible remedies:

- *Compensation:* Employees should be paid a fair wage or salary in return for the services expected from them and the responsibilities assigned. This should be based upon competitive research and the consequence of error. A higher consequence of error can result in a higher monetary penalty for the company if a mistake is made in that position. A higher level of competency is required to fill such a position and there is a price attached to find a qualified individual. One of the primary motivating factors for employees is money; therefore, a performance based bonus structure rewards high producing employees and leaves mediocre workers with their base salary only and no one else to blame. This method of compensation may take some creativity in determining a measuring tool as most goals require numbers and a specified time period.

- *Coaching vs. Managing:* Managers implement company policy and ensure that departments function to meet company objectives. This is generally done without compassion, not always a motivating way to run a company from an employee perspective, but often necessary to stay in business. Coaching and mentoring are motivating and nurturing terms that should become an important addition to the dictionary of entrepreneurs who have employees in their charge. The autocratic management technique that adopts, *"My way or the highway,"* does not motivate people or encourage productivity. There is a great deal of excellent material available on this subject.

- *Unrealistic Expectations:* It is a common practice for many small business owners to expect that employees can match their own abilities and learn the processes to the same level. Every person operates at a different speed with a different capacity for learning. The maximum performance, productivity and attainable levels of achievement will be different with each individual operating at their own one hundred percent output level. These limitations must be recognized quickly by the entrepreneur and employees requiring repetition of simple tasks to learn must be mentored patiently. These individuals can be very reliable and productive members of an organization's work force and should be rewarded when they achieve levels consistent with their own maximum effort.

- *Micro Managing:* It is human nature for small business owners to micro manage their business. After all, it is your baby and no one can do the job (*any job*) as well as you. Right? This form of managing a business works fine with most clerical and general labor positions where the employee requires guidance and expects to be given direction regularly. The problem really surfaces when a management position is added, such as illustrated in the org chart, *Fig. 4.1 – Year Five.* At this stage the owner is compensating a highly skilled and experienced person to make certain decisions. Although it is difficult to let go, second guessing and always looking over the shoulder of a person delegated to make decisions is not only de-motivating but belittling as well and this treatment almost always results in the loss of good people.

- *Buy In:* Most small business decisions are made without employee input. They are told that this is the way it is going to be, "Here is the company policy and it is expected that you will follow it without question." The new duties will generally be performed according to policy but if there is no clear understanding, if there is a disbelief in the reasoning behind a decision, the result will be a lack of enthusiasm and performance will suffer. Employees cannot have a say in critical business issues such as financial management; however, certain marketing and operational decisions can benefit from front line input and instill pride of ownership. Employees will always look for more efficient ways to complete a task and their input can improve an organization's bottom line if a better process is adopted. Many innovative companies, like *3M*, have encouraged employees to suggest ideas for new products and they are rewarded handsomely if a product goes to market. Post this point with a *sticky note*!

When Things Go Bad

It will not always be the case that you are going to bring an employee on board who will be a perfect fit for the company, exceed all expectations and prove to be completely reliable. Mistakes are going to be made in the selection process where candidates that are less than ideal will be offered positions. As with any other type of planning, the more scrutiny afforded the process, the less likelihood that trouble will show up at 9am to sour the company culture and environment. On occasion, an employee who has a good work history can turn for no apparent reason and become a liability. This is generally due to personal problems or an incident in the workplace that turned their feelings about the company or fellow workers. There are also certain behaviors where any employee can be terminated on the spot for cause.

Probationary Employees

It is much easier to terminate a probationary employee during the first three months for performance issues or being a poor fit for the company. Firing someone is one of the hardest things a business owner will do. Unfortunately, it is business and if they will not work out then cut your losses and end the anxiety that the employee must be feeling as well. If it appears that the new employee can still make the grade with more assistance, and they have the desire to succeed, it may be worth having them agree to an extension of the probationary period. It is much more difficult to terminate a problem employee for performance issues after this period.

Permanent Employees

Poor performance, increased absenteeism, and complaining are signs of a problem that must be addressed immediately. The first step is to bring the situation to the employee's attention during a private meeting. Try to identify the problem with a resolution offering assistance where required. Keep in mind that family will always come first. Complaining is a terrible disease of the workplace that must be stopped or removed before it spreads to other employees. As with performance issues, give the problem worker a written letter outlining the problem, the desired outcome, and the time period for re-evaluation. It should be noted that the performance or behavior is contrary to the terms of employment. It should also be made clear if the behavior is disruptive, that failure to improve may result in termination. If the letter is a result of performance issues, it should also indicate how the company plans to assist them. If the poor performance persists, another letter re-stating the problem, expected results, and time period along with a notation that termination may be the result should be delivered. In all instances, take detailed notes and file every document in the employee's personal file. You may need to show all of the steps and the opportunities afforded them to succeed in the event of litigation. At times it may be prudent to have another person sit in for the interview. This person should preferably be in management and not a co-worker.

(Review your termination procedure requirements with your lawyer to ensure adherence to labor legislation.)

4.3.3 Employee Relations Dos and Don'ts

- *Do* - develop a good plan for recruiting and training new employees.

- *Do* - create a detailed job description for each position within the company and when the staff number grows beyond five, develop an employee handbook, including a Code of Conduct.

- *Do* - try to develop a performance based compensation plan. This is generally a bonus structure that is paid in addition to base salary for individual personal or team goal achievement. Since goals require numbers and a time frame for measurement, some employee performance levels are difficult to judge objectively. Unlike sales people who have assigned revenue quotas, clerical employees or line workers have duties that are much harder to quantify. Consider other areas of productivity if necessary, such as quality control levels, customer service recognition or team efforts that have a positive impact on the company's profitability.

- *Do* - learn to coach and mentor employees.

- *Do* - provide workers with a safe and healthy environment.

- *Do* - provide the tools, equipment, training and assistance to allow employees to reach their full potential.

- *Do* - recognize and reward outstanding performance and achievements.

- *Do* - use compassion when handling certain personal and family issues.

- *Do* - use firmness along with decisiveness when required for issues that could have a negative effect on the operations of the business.

- *Do* - use good negotiation skills when dealing with employee friction. It is human nature that personality clashes will occur when people spend so much of their time together with co-workers. Always strive for a *win – win* outcome and ask questions to ensure the combatants' inclusion in the solution, stressing the benefits for the company, team and individuals.

- *Don't* - tolerate any type of behavior that may have an adverse effect on morale. The worst of these are complaining and the spreading of rumors. Both activities will propagate a negative atmosphere quickly and even de-motivate your best employees. Deal with this one as soon as it surfaces.

- *Don't* - allow any form of discrimination, violence, sexual harassment or human rights violations to occur in the workplace. Adopt a zero tolerance policy and make it clear in the handbook.

- *Don't* - reprimand or discipline an employee in front of associates. With the exception of providing praise or recognition, deal with employees in private.

- *Don't* - reprimand an employee or deal with a difficult person while angry. This will most often result in words being spoken by both parties that will be regretted. It is best to sleep on it, and then investigate the incident. Send the employee home for the rest of the day if necessary until all parties involved have cooled down. There are two sides to every coin, yet many managers often listen to a complaint then immediately pass judgement or draw a conclusion, often false.

4.4 Contingency Planning

Why do stores sell out of generators the day after a major power outage? Or snow blowers the day after the season's biggest snowfall? Or air conditioners on the last day of a long heat spell? This scenario repeats itself over and over in many other situations – not just the examples mentioned. It is called being reactive versus proactive. It is only natural for us to relax our guard and become complacent after a period of calm. Working for someone else allows a certain level of complacency, confident that the boss has prepared for unforeseen circumstances and emergencies. As a business owner, letting your guard down could have disastrous consequences and possibly put you out of business. The events of 9/11 have changed the way we travel, the political landscape and the way we look at business security. A number of unfortunate companies lost everything that fateful day. However, due to thorough continuity planning and contingency preparedness, many were up and running within hours from another location with current back up records and a plan. Large public corporations update emergency planning and run drills because of awareness, and more importantly, because the shareholders demand it to protect their investment. Unfortunately, this is an area that does not receive the attention it deserves from small business owners due to complacency, lack of knowledge and a common reactive nature.

An example of the type of catastrophe that could hit any small business, described as follows, is based on a true occurrence. One October evening a series of severe thunderstorms ripped through the city outskirts with a high level of ground to cloud lightning activity. The small office building took a direct hit from a powerful strike that arced into the electrical circuit powering the computers in one of the offices. The equipment was plugged in to APC surge protection/ battery *backups*, however, the charge was so powerful that these units instantly fried and the current continued its split second advance through computers, printers and all peripheral hardware destroying mother boards and hard drives including all data. The charge continued through the network cable to the other two offices housing computer equipment with the same instant destruction and located a phone line plugged into a modem leading the surge to more circuits.

Now travelling unrestricted through the phone and three electrical circuits, the blast hit the main panel blowing breakers, the telephone distribution panel and the alarm system panel which set off the siren. The devastating force terminated at the hydro pole on the street where the transformer lid was blown fifty feet in the air.

The business owner was contacted by the alarm monitoring station that received a warning for a broken phone connection at the location. Upon arrival, the shocked entrepreneur entered the smoky building to the acrid smell of burning electronic circuitry. Luckily there was no structural fire; however, the extent of damage was staggering: four computers, three printers, scanners, fax machine and copier, APC backups, complete telephone and alarm system, ALL data and software on hard drives including complete customer databases, correspondence, and accounting data. Imagine yourself in this situation – one of many potentially catastrophic situations that can occur without notice. What would you do? If you are like many reactive small business owners, this loss of data could seriously jeopardize the continuity of the company.

Fortunately, this proactive business person was constantly thinking ahead and planning for the worst case scenario. Computer hardware was replaced within forty-eight hours and all electrical, telephone, and alarm circuitry was repaired or replaced in the same time frame. Although computer hard drives were destroyed along with the data stored on them, it wasn't a great concern as the company had adopted a very rigid data backup regimen with secure storage on and off site. Even if the building had burned to the ground, the data could still be retrieved. Although inconvenient, software was reloaded along with the data and operations were completely back to normal within seventy-two hours. Since the owner had a more than adequate small business insurance plan, all of the equipment and repairs were covered.

Large enterprises can afford to bring in experts for a risk analysis and audit, contingency planning then testing. Public companies must engage in continuity assurances as ISO standards and shareholder interests must be honored. All small enterprises can guarantee business continuity in an emergency by following a few simple steps without incurring a high expense. The process is not difficult, but it can be time consuming initially to identify all areas of business operations that can be affected. Once these areas are identified, a plan can be drafted with remedies for recovery and continuity that include: emergency numbers and contact names, a list of persons responsible for executing the plan, and duties to be completed. When the detailed contingency plan has been developed, it should be re-visited at regular time intervals to ensure that the information is up to date, and the execution of the action plan meets expectations.

A simple method that can be utilized for small business contingency planning is to examine all of your business processes and apply the **what if** scenario to each. This will identify potentially vulnerable areas that require attention. Most contingency issues concern the processes of the internal environment, so deal with this area first. There are numerous input and output functions that operate internally in any organization. For this example, our audit will include production, administration, and human resources.

Internal Business Environment

Production and Facility

What are some of the areas of production that can be affected? Make a list. They may include facility. Start applying the *what if* test to every aspect of facility. These are only sample questions. Determine those applicable to your own company that may or may not be on this suggested list.

- When does the **lease expire**? Will the landlord renew or raise the price?

  Define a timetable to negotiate a lease renewal with the landlord or set a date to begin a search for a new facility if negotiations fail.

- If there is a fire, loss, or damage, is the **insurance coverage** adequate?

  Check all perils covered by the policy and deductibles. Keep in mind if you operate out of a home office that most home insurance policies do not cover business losses. Additional policy riders will be necessary.

- If equipment requires repair or replacement, is there a **secondary resource**?

  The original supplier of a critical piece of production equipment may not be in business when it breaks down. If this holds up production, it will definitely result in lost revenue, but also lost customers. Search out backup sources of parts and maintenance.

- If there is a lengthy **power interruption**, what is the cost in lost production?

It may be necessary to purchase a backup generator. If your company operates in the food industry at any level, a backup system is necessary if there are frozen or perishable items involved.

- If a primary supplier goes out of business, is there a secondary source for the supply of **raw materials**?

  The rule here, as in other aspects of business – "Do not put all of your eggs in one basket!" Running out of production supply puts an immediate stop to output with a terrible impact on all company stakeholders. Check often for new areas of supply and utilize some of them occasionally for small purchases in case the favorite goes out of business. It is also important to shop around regularly for the best price and quality to maintain healthy margins and remain highly competitive.

Examine warehousing, licensing, vehicles and any other area you can think of within the production category applying the worst case scenario test to each.

Administration - IT

This area covers many processes such as accounting and finance along with the hardware and software that powers it.

- If there was a fire, explosion, tornado or lightning strike, how soon could **hardware** be replaced and systems restored? Is **software** ready to re-install?

  o *Keep a record of all model and serials numbers, purchase price, place of purchase and date of purchase. Although equipment is depreciated on the books every year, insurance generally includes a replacement cost provision. Maintain a folder with the bill of sale, owner's manual, and warranty cards. (Don't forget to register your products with the manufacturer – if all else fails they will generally have a record of your equipment with all information in their database. Keep serial / model numbers in MS Excel or Word as well.)*

  o *Software will need to be loaded into the new computers if there is total damage to the electronics. Keep all original installing media in a safe place along with the serial numbers or key codes. Most licensing allows for a single duplicate – keep the copy off site along with the serial number. Register the software with the developer – again, if all else fails and your programs are lost in a fire, there will be a record to obtain replacements. This registration process is also important for technical support and discounted upgrades when new versions are released.*

- Are data backups being performed properly?

Backing up data on a hard drive is an automatic process with most programs. It is surprising to find the number of people who believe this is adequate. Hardware does age, like everything else, and crashes (*and lightning strikes*) do happen. Software can easily be re-installed in new computers if necessary – data is another story. The programs are not your business, but the data is, and without it, any business is in big trouble! Adopting a proper back up procedure is imperative for business continuity. Keeping data stored on external media will not help if the building burns to the ground. The amazing technology available today makes it possible to back up a complete hard drive on a memory stick. One back up copy should be kept in the office and another kept off site. This can be done as easily as taking a data memory stick or external drive home with you or even using an out source or on-line data back service. The important message here is to ensure that the data (*your business lifeline*) is current and available in any situation.

o *Accounting data should be backed up after each session. These are your key business finance files and, at minimum, there should be a disc for each fiscal quarter and the year end with a copy stored off site.*

o *Data Base files can be a different story depending upon the size of your business and the volume of daily activity. Data base files can become corrupted in a number of ways, rendering certain files useless. They must be overwritten with a recent clean back up file and there will be a loss of data between the date of corruption and the date of the restored file. Daily back up is a good habit for all data; however, if this back up continually overwrites the activity from the previous day, it is possible that a clean file will not be available to replace one that becomes corrupt. The answer for low volume activity is to perform the back up on four media, each corresponding to the weeks of the month. If a file is lost in week four, it can be replaced with a file from week three or two without a catastrophic loss of data. For companies with a high level of database activity, a media for each day of the month is an absolute must. Offsite storage is also a necessity along with the typical media storage in the office.*

o *Document folders containing word processing, spreadsheet, image and graphic files must also be backed up on a regular basis on and off site. The complete company web site, as described in Section 4.2, should be protected in the same way.*

Human Resources

HR is another internal process that requires scrutiny, not only for the safety of employees and visitors to your facility, but also to avoid heavy fines and negative public branding.

- If there was an **accident**, is the company prepared?

    o *Ensure that there are enough employees trained in first aid to guarantee that a qualified individual is working at all times and only minutes away when needed to render assistance.*

    o *Check that there is a fully stocked first aid station and assign someone to check the supplies on a regular basis. This can be outsourced.*

    o *Create a safety team to check and enforce safety standards.*

    o *Conduct regular fire drills.*

- Is there total compliance with all **employee legislated** departments and organizations?

    o *Workplace Health and Safety regulations must be adhered to. It is the employer's responsibility to make the workplace safe so that each employee can count on returning home safely to their family every day. Hazardous materials must be properly marked and handled. Employees must be trained in their safe handling and where required, appropriate permits and certification must be acquired. Design an emergency material handling plan and conduct drills regularly.*

    o *Worker's Compensation coverage must be adequate in the case of a workplace accident.*

- If the company lost a **key employee**, has someone else been trained to take their place?

Cross training is an effective way to ensure that important positions can always be filled and essential duties completed. Also, consider a Key Person insurance plan if the company would suffer serious hardship with the loss of an individual.

External Business Environment

Business Travel

There are only a few issues that may be of concern in the external environment. One of them is business travel.

- Are there any ***security*** issues in the countries where key personnel are scheduled to travel?

  If there are issues, plan ahead by getting country reports from the Foreign Affairs department web site. Many large companies contract security firms to provide close protection to their key management personnel at home and abroad.

- Do key individuals ***travel together?***

  Complete management teams have been lost to companies from plane crashes resulting in a difficult period of rebuilding and vulnerability.

Marketing

- If the company lost one of its ***largest customers***, what would the impact be on annual sales?

  Look at the percentage of your annual revenue that is attached to your largest customers. If all of your eggs are in one basket, contingency planning is a must. Should your key sales contact with the largest customer be replaced by someone who uses competitive products, it could mean the end for your main source of revenue. Start cultivating relationships with more decision making and influencing individuals within the customer's management team.

- Is there pending **government legislation** that could influence business operations? Is the company prepared for any outcome in advance?

  This can be a difficult question to answer. The best way to learn of pending legislation or events is through an industry association. A person in the company should be assigned to stay on top of this issue if your industry can be affected. An example of this was the legislation passed in many states and provinces that banned radar detection devices. Numerous companies went out of business as this was their only product.

The list can go on as you examine all of your business processes. Put every "*what if*" on paper and include for each an action and the name of the person assigned the responsibility of implementation. Review each "*what if*" with any individuals who may be directly involved with the outcome. This method of planning can be applied to almost any business of any size. More resources are available on the Internet using a search for the keywords *Contingency Planning* and *Business Continuity Planning.*

conclusion

We have seen that business ownership is full of risks and is not for everyone. For the select few who possess the character and resources to become entrepreneurs, many personal and monetary rewards await the individuals who are successful. The rewards are not exclusive to the men and women who operate small business. We are all rewarded by their achievements as small enterprise drives the national economy, is the largest employer and a major catalyst for innovation.

Proper planning cannot eliminate the risk associated with small business ownership but can reduce it substantially. In order to generate the income necessary to sustain business operations and growth, an effective marketing strategy must be developed and delivered as detailed in Section 2. Financial mismanagement as outlined in Section 3 must be avoided above all to remain profitable. If one part of this book has assisted in helping an entrepreneur avoid a pitfall, or develop better habits leading to more profit, then I have succeeded in the goal established when I set out to write *The Small Business Planner*.

Readers are urged to take advantage of the business templates that have been created, available for free download from the companion web site, www.consultbiz.net. This site was developed for *The Small Business Planner* community along with a forum to share ideas and solutions for others. With success comes responsibility, not only to your stakeholders, but foremost to your family, the community in which you operate, and those truly in need who deserve generosity. To make this happen, the successful entrepreneur must also be responsible to themselves in maintaining a healthy lifestyle including proper nutrition, activity and rest.

Be passionate—be profitable—make it happen!

resources

The files included with this book are protected by Copyright© for the sole use of the purchaser and may not be copied for circulation or distributed to other persons.

MS Word documents and templates are provided in *Word 97 – 2003* .doc format. (*They will open with all of these versions of MS Word*) Simply overwrite the existing text and add your own information to maintain formatting. The complete business plan requires the marketing plan as an insert at the appropriate section.

Business Plan

Marketing Plan

MS Excel worksheets are provided in *Excel 97 – 2003* .xls format. (*They will open with all of these versions of MS Excel from 97 to 2007*). These worksheets are complete with formulas where possible and they are fully customizable to suit your own company requirements. Replace any sample data with your own company figures and delete or insert rows as required.

Profit and Loss Projection

Cash Flow Projection

Start-Up Cost Worksheet

Variance Analysis Worksheet

Competitive Analysis Worksheet

Media Plan Worksheet

Sales Call Sheets *(one for a single week, month, and quarter)*

Template downloads are free and available on the companion web site, **www.consultbiz.net** along with many other business planning resources. These include a Bulletin Board for sharing ideas and posting questions. Registration is required (free) to log in and use these resources.

about the author

larry wilson has a highly diversified background. After completing high school he joined the police force and quickly climbed the ranks, spending much of his career in criminal investigation. During his fourteen years on the force, he also attended university working toward a degree in economics while earning two degrees in police sciences. He conceded to his entrepreneurial spirit and started his own business in publishing, then graphic arts. After learning some valuable business lessons, the author decided to join the white collar ranks of big business and took a sales role in financial services. During his first three years successfully selling consumer solutions, he also studied sales skills at colleges in Ontario and California. He next accepted a position with a leading supplier of business accounts receivable services. After quickly becoming the top Canadian sales person, a promotion to sales management was followed with a company take-over by the largest international player in personal and now business credit reporting services. A promotion after the take-over to regional sales management, then manager of a key business unit, gave him the experience to later provide a complete package of business consulting services to clients. This was combined with further university studies in marketing and organizational behavior along with numerous computer training courses and a *Microsoft Office User Expert* certification. When the company decided to down size the commercial sales division, the author opted again for entrepreneurship and started his management consulting practice specializing in marketing and small business technology. He also started a successful Internet travel business.

In addition to providing general business consulting services to private sector clients, a government sponsored business program near Toronto, Ontario contracted his services for a mentoring program helping budding entrepreneurs in the development of business plans. He also assisted a new business centre in Barrie, Ontario, in the complete development of a program for business start-ups, and a number of seminars were created that covered all aspects of business planning and marketing, including web development. In a five year period, over 500 new businesses received his assistance in business plan development and a number of them were honored for achievement by local chambers of commerce. During this time, the author also taught business courses and web development at Georgian College for part-time studies and wrote a monthly column in a regional business newspaper.

His company provides complete marketing and Internet solutions for small businesses. The author has developed and delivers popular seminars based upon sections of *The Small Business Planner* including the *Ten Most Common Marketing Mistakes* and *Developing Effective Business Web Sites.* He continues to work with entrepreneurs in mentoring programs and currently lives in Central Ontario cottage country with his wife, enjoying the seasons and the great outdoors.

INDEX

P

BUY A SHARE OF THE FUTURE IN YOUR COMMUNITY

These certificates make great holiday, graduation and birthday gifts that can be personalized with the recipient's name. The cost of one S.H.A.R.E. or one square foot is $54.17. The personalized certificate is suitable for framing and will state the number of shares purchased and the amount of each share, as well as the recipient's name. The home that you participate in "building" will last for many years and will continue to grow in value.

HABITAT FOR HUMANITY

THIS CERTIFIES THAT

YOUR NAME HERE

HAS INVESTED IN A HOME FOR A DESERVING FAMILY

1985-2010

TWENTY-FIVE YEARS OF BUILDING FUTURES
IN OUR COMMUNITY ONE HOME AT A TIME

1200 SQUARE FOOT HOUSE @ $65,000 = $54.17 PER SQUARE FOOT
This certificate represents a tax deductible donation. It has no cash value.

Here is a sample SHARE certificate:

YES, I WOULD LIKE TO HELP!

I support the work that Habitat for Humanity does and I want to be part of the excitement! As a donor, I will receive periodic updates on your construction activities but, more importantly, I know my gift will help a family in our community realize the dream of homeownership. **I would like to SHARE in your efforts against substandard housing in my community!** *(Please print below)*

PLEASE SEND ME _____ SHARES at $54.17 EACH = $ $_____

In Honor Of: _____

Occasion: (Circle One)   HOLIDAY   BIRTHDAY   ANNIVERSARY

     OTHER: _____

Address of Recipient: _____

Gift From: _____ *Donor Address:* _____

Donor Email: _____

I AM ENCLOSING A CHECK FOR $ $_____ PAYABLE TO HABITAT FOR HUMANITY <u>OR</u> PLEASE CHARGE MY VISA OR MASTERCARD *(CIRCLE ONE)*

Card Number _____ Expiration Date: _____

Name as it appears on Credit Card _____ Charge Amount $ _____

Signature _____

Billing Address _____

Telephone # Day _____ Eve _____

PLEASE NOTE: Your contribution is tax-deductible to the fullest extent allowed by law.
Habitat for Humanity • P.O. Box 1443 • Newport News, VA 23601 • 757-596-5553
www.HelpHabitatforHumanity.org

CPSIA information can be obtained at www.ICGtesting.com
Printed in the USA
LVOW041209301011

252706LV00004B/44/P